So
Swift
the
Storm

So Swift the Storm

LaJoyce Martin

So Swift The Storm

By LaJoyce Martin

©1990 Word Aflame Press
Hazelwood, MO 63042-2299
Printing History: 1994, 1996

Cover Design by Tim Agnew

All Scripture quotations in this book are from the King James Version of the Bible unless otherwise identified.

Printed in United States of America.

Printed by

Library of Congress Cataloging-in-Publication Data

Martin, LaJoyce, 1937-
    So Swift the storm / by LaJoyce Martin.
        p.   cm.
    ISBN 0-932581-66-8 :
    I. Title.
PS3563.A72486S6   1990
813'.54--dc20   90-35201
                                                                      CIP

To My First Grandchild

Table of Contents

1

The Sandstorm

A rusty cloud squatted on the horizon.
"A bad sandstorm's a-comin', Maw." The ten-year-old boy threw the urgent words and a limber, scrawny cat through the open front door.

"Pen up th' animals, Willy." The large woman lifted vacant black eyes and turned toward Anna. "And Anna, you get th' clothes off th' line."

"Yes'm." The girl got up from her darning, pushed aside her mending basket, and moved toward the barren back yard.

Choking sand, marshaled from miles around, would soon whip around the windows and doors searing any surfaces it touched, piling into deep drifts, and leaving bare feet to suffer its sandpaper abrasion on the floors—if one was fortunate enough to have floors. Anna shuddered. *The worst part,* she thought, *is the gritty feeling on your teeth.* She hated it all.

Inside, young Willy worried on. "But what about Paw and Jason, Maw? What if they get caught out in it? It's easy to get yourself lost when th' sand covers over th' roads. You can't tell where you're goin'."

"They're both of age, Willy, and reasonably intelligent. They'll stop off somewhere in a protected place," his mother said.

Anna studied the low, red menace boiling higher and higher in the western sky. An hour, maybe two. . . . Her arms reached for the threadbare towels, tie-dyed to match the iron in the water. With the choice of a whole nation of virgin land, she could not imagine why anyone would chose to live on these high, windblown plains. Yet her family had lived here for as long as she could remember. And what progress had they made?

She supposed, weary thought, that she would finish out her monotonous existence right here in the timeworn pattern of day and night, sleeping and waking, winter and summer—and sandstorms. Stuck in a muddy backwash with no movement or change, she would watch the current of life pass her by.

The rattle of a wagon pulled her vision across the treeless distance to a familiar sight. It would be her father and Jason hurrying home to beat the blinding sand. They'd been to Lubbock for supplies.

"Maw!" Anna heard Willy shout. "Here comes Paw and Jason now! They're just ahead of th' storm!"

She must have seen the second wagon about the time Willy spied it. "And Maw! There's another wagon follerin' behind. And it looks *newer* and *bigger*. Surely Paw didn't buy us *another* wagon, did he?"

Corine Lewis was at the door shading her eyes with a fleshy hand, a habit of hers whether the sun glared or not. "No, Willy. Your father hadn't th' money to buy another wagon. And if he did have that kind of money, he'd best be buyin' something different than another

10

wagon or I'd be raisin' Cain and he'd be takin' it right
back where he got it from."

"Then who'd be th' other wagon, Maw?"

"Someone just passin', Willy."

Anna watched the wagons snake their way across the
sage-dotted prairie toward the adobe shack. Relief that
her father and brother were safe was her sole emotion.
Especially was she grateful for the homecoming of Jason,
her older brother. He had taken her part against her un-
reasonable mother more than once in the past few weeks.
He was her anchorage. If anything happened to him . . .

A prickling, like a grassburr that clung to her worn
skirt and snagged now and then on her patched cotton
stockings, scratched at her mind. The age-old question
came back to torment her. Why did her mother resent
her presence in the home? Why would one have a child
if she didn't *want* that child? Any resemblance between
mother and daughter was nonexistent, in looks or attitude. Anna's fair-skinned beauty and gentle spirit made
a ridiculous yokefellow for Corine Lewis's coarse features
and bitter tongue. And what of her silent father? Why
had he never taken her part? Was it his love for peace
or Corine's domination that tied his tongue for offense
or defense?

Jason was a tall, handsome brother with clear, honest
eyes that any seventeen-year-old sister could be proud of.
And proud of him she was! They'd had precious few opportunities for personal talks over the years—her mother
saw to that—but once Jason put his hand on her thin shoulder and said, "Anna, you are a brave girl. I want you to
marry a man worthy of you. *Honest* men are few and far
between. But don't settle for less. Whatever you do, don't

11

let Maw pawn you off on the first rat that comes blowing across the desert."

His lips smiled down at her from his towering height, but she read concern in his brown eyes. "I'll probably never marry, Jason," she said. "Where would I find anyone to marry in this forsaken land? But thanks for your . . . trust in me."

"Someday I'll have a job of my own, little sister. I'll see that you have your chance." His voice almost broke with the conviction of the words. "I'll buy you a new dress and take you into town with me. . . ."

That's all the conversation there had been time for. Corine Lewis appeared from nowhere and demanded work instead of idleness of Anna, using a few choice words to establish her point. Then with her surplus rage, she swore at the cat. Had Jason's rush of sympathy, smothered with emotion, been overheard by his mother?

Each time Jason championed her cause, the friction between mother and daughter intensified. Anna wanted to ask her brother many questions: Why did her mother distrust her, exclude her from her affections, give her so little consideration?

If she had been a boy, she decided, instead of a female child, things would have been different. At least somewhat different. Jason merited a small degree of Corine's devotion, but young Willy was his mother's idol, blotting up her attention.

Several small graves, like earth malignancies, formed mounds on the prairie, all within the perimeter of Anna's memory. They had been boys, too premature to live but a few hours. One was buried when she was five, another when she was nine, another at twelve, and the last death came two years ago when she was fifteen. Only Willy had miraculously lived to absorb his mother's interest.

Anna shed few tears for her siblings' untimely births. She embraced Job's philosophy that such fortunate souls merely escaped the toils of this present life. Given a choice, she would gladly have died and allowed one of the boys to live in her stead. Surely her mother, with her partiality for male children, would have preferred it.

The wagons drew in. Anna expected the second wagon to move on past the stucco house, but it did not. The driver reined up alongside the Lewis rig.

Willy bolted out the door, his freckled face split with a grin of welcome for whomever the visitors might be. A sanguine chap, he loved the whole of humanity. Corine stood in the opening, her orb-shaped face expressionless.

"You'd best not try to go on until th' storm passes," Mr. Lewis told the driver. "These West Texas sandstorms ain't no picnic. We'll put you up for the night. Let's get ever'body safe inside. It'll hit ere long, and she looks like a wicked demon."

At first Anna thought that the conveyance belched out three full-grown travelers. Then she saw that the one woman among the trio grasped a bundle close to her body. It could be bedding—or it could be a child.

As the tall woman moved toward the house, Anna decided that the roll must be extra clothing. Her wrinkled face and graying hair would surely put her outside the age bracket of motherhood. She must be well past fifty.

Frequent short looks kept Anna's curiosity from becoming an open stare. The lady's grand dress, of faded lavender taffeta, rippled out in the back over a rumpled

13

bustle. Up behind the wearer's large ears, a high boned collar fanned out. The finery spoke of a world unknown to the prairie-grown girl. Each time she glanced away, the magnet of girlish marvel brought her eyes back again to weave a score of fanciful stories.

Then the lady traveler uncovered the fuzzy head of a very young baby who set up a chronic fret, smacking at its tiny fingers.

Hypnotized with the irony of an aged mother and a young infant, Anna hardly took notice of the men, one of whom was about Jason's age. The older, taller man bent down to get through the doorway, a low-linteled opening that lacked two or three inches of doubling a yardstick. A gravelly voice took custody of her attention.

"The name's Horn, madam. Philip, it is." The senior of the two folded in the middle in a sort of bow to Corine Lewis. His small black mustache, drooping and sparse, seemed out of proportion to the rest of his face. "The wife here is Esther. And this is our son, Lesley. Hope we don't inconvenience you too sorely. Your good husband insisted we lodge here until the storm passes over." He made no mention of the baby as if it did not exist.

Anna blushed when she realized that Lesley Horn's keen eyes were upon her, appraising her. She looked down, but not before her swift glance caught Jason's face. It wore a dark, angry expression. She was aware, with chagrin, that her mother's eyes missed none of the action. What it all meant she did not know. She would have to wait until later to take the wrappings off the mystery to see it better.

"Have you bedding in th' wagon, Mr. Horn?" Richard Lewis asked.

"Yes, sir."

"Then we'd best get it before th' sand does. We'll likely be needing it for pallets th' night."

The two men moved out with urgent haste, but Lesley made no effort to join them. Anna battled with a disquieting sensation as the young man still stared at her. Her sixth sense told her that nothing had changed: his hungry eyes, Jason's black wrath, or Corine's watchful surveillance. But she dared not look.

The plaintive cries of the child grew more frantic, its scanty stock of patience sabotaged by the discomforts of hunger.

"Have you any milk to spare, Mrs. Lewis?" Esther's eyes and voice held a plea. "The baby has had nothing but water for hours."

"Goat's milk. Heat some goat's milk for th' baby, Anna."

Anna's body moved in wordless obedience.

"The baby has been sick a great deal," Esther said. "It's a girl-child. We still don't know if she will be strong enough to make this trip to the end. We haven't named her yet. What's the use naming a little thing that's here today and gone tomorrow?" She focused tired gray eyes on Corine. But Corine only bunched her shoulders in a noncommittal shrug. Anna wondered if her mother's memories were too raw to trust herself with a verbal response to Esther's questioning.

"The babe's mother died on the journey," continued Esther in a matter-of-fact voice, giving the impression that grief took too much effort. "We buried her beside the road. This is my son's baby."

Anna, busy at the stove, cast a quick, involuntary

15

glance at Lesley. He shot his mother a glare akin to hatred. She supposed he had not wished the personal information about himself disclosed. If his mother caught the undertow, she chose to ignore it.

"Your son isn't very old." Corine's tongue seemed to speak by itself.

"Lesley's twenty-four."

"One year older than my Jason."

"Lesley's wife was about the same age. We never knew *exactly* how old she was."

"Her Maw didn't keep no records?"

"She was an orphan."

"I see."

Under dipped lashes, Anna looked around. Lesley's sardonic smirk reflected a deformed soul given to evil humor. She could not identify his expression by conscious thought, only with her spirit. She wanted to run, to escape. Jason still nurtured his silent smolder. Corine and Esther seemed to divine the dangerous toxin between their two sons and tried to wash it away with the purgative of their prattle. But the strain hung in the air like deadly fumes.

"Take this bottle to the girl, Lesley." Esther slipped her hand into her pocket and produced a dirty, crooknecked bottle. "Please wash it out good before you put the milk in it, miss."

"You might help your father, Jason." Corine's suggestion carried the connotation of a command. But Jason kept his eyes glued upon Lesley, scorning his mother's instructions.

Anna took the bottle, avoiding eye contact with Lesley and taking great care that their hands not meet. His strange, intent stare made her skin prickle. A nameless shame sent hot waves up her neck.

The warm milk soothed the child and she fell asleep. "May I lay her down, Mrs. Lewis? I've held her in my arms for hours," Esther said. In answer, Corine pointed to Anna's bunk in the curtained-off room no larger than a closet.

The sandstorm hit, a mad blizzard of flying dust mingled with dried grass, racing tumbleweeds, and cacti. The sun, obscured by the fury, turned to a plate of pale yellow, bringing eerie darkness. Corine lighted a lamp. Its smoky tasty smell filled the room, and a jagged flame gradually adjusted to clear gold as Corine rolled the wick up and then down again. She swiped at the tin reflector with a soiled cloth in an effort to coax all the light possible from the vapid lantern.

When breathing became laborious, Anna and her father wetted rags and gave to the guests to put over their nostrils. Anna found herself wondering if the poor, weak baby could survive in the stifling air.

"How . . . long . . . does . . . it . . . last?" gasped Philip Horn above the awful roar of the wind.

"Usually no more than three or four hours. But it could last all night." Richard Lewis took the cloth from his nose long enough to answer.

Anna tried to find a place to sit out of Lesley's direct range of vision. In the small room, it wasn't easy. When he purposely moved, Jason arranged his split-bottom chair so as to block the young man's view of his sister. Anna smiled a thanks to her brother. He tilted his head in acknowledgement but gave her no smile in return. His locked jaw muscles suggested hard-set teeth. Why was her brother so angry?

17

The howling of the wind grew wilder as whipping flurries and gusts wrapped the house in a veil beyond which none could see. Anna blinked to keep the fine sand from biting at her dry eyeballs. She had lived through many such sandstorms but never became accustomed to their blazing, parching terror. She thanked God for the protection of thin mud walls, knowing that those less fortunate who were caught outside would be battered with glasslike particles powerful enough to bring the blood to one's unprotected cheeks.

Night drew on, and in the drowning fog of thick dust, each found a place to sleep amid the grit and grime. Anna offered her bed to Esther and the baby. "I'll sit the night," she offered. She reasoned that with Lesley Horn in the house she would feel safer sitting up anyway. She associated Lesley with some unspeakable danger.

Esther placed her mouth close to Anna's ear. "Would you mind to hold the baby for me awhile tonight and let me sleep?" she whispered. "I haven't had a night's rest since my daughter-in-law died and left me with the burden."

Anna's eyes widened in fright; she had never held a baby. Her own mother did not trust her with any of the ill-fated brothers. And what if the sick child should die in her arms? She started to object, but Esther must have read her thoughts. "You'll do fine with her. With all that rich milk in her belly, she won't die before morning."

Anna took the baby, the bottle, and two gauzy dishtowels converted to diapers. She expected her mother to snatch the infant from her arms, protesting that she was not responsible enough to care for a child so fragile, but she did not.

18

The child was so small, so helpless. And so . . . *un-wanted,* Anna thought. Lesley hardly offered his daughter a passing glance. To her own grandmother, the baby was a burden. Her grandfather acted as though she did not exist. Tears of pity slid from Anna's red-rimmed and bloodshot eyes onto the newborn's inadequate wrap. She pulled the tiny body close and pressed wind-cracked lips into the soft down of hair. "I could love you," she murmured. "You and I have something in common. No one really cares what happens to either of us." At the sound of the crooning, the child began to relax against Anna's shoulder.

The storm finished its savage tantrum about midnight, spent and gone. The worn travelers slept, while Anna swayed back and forth to solace the little one. In a half-sleep dream, the two of them seemed to be abandoned in a great wilderness and she fought off wild beasts that would take the child from her.

Before dawn, someone touched her shoulder and she jumped, frozen into panic with the thought that it might be Lesley. But Lesley slept like one drugged, caring for nothing except his own comforts. It was Jason who came to suggest that she take his pallet and let him sit awhile. She thought to refuse, but her arms, unaccustomed to the weight, ached and her bones cried for a place to stretch out. So she laid down behind a flimsy curtain with the unnamed baby on her chest and slept as if she would never move again.

The sun rose in a blue, clear sky. The air was startlingly fresh and clean, all traces of its sand-spitting fit gone. The baby drew a long, sighing breath, rousing Anna. From beyond the jerry-built curtain, the sound of two

19

hushed voices reached her ears.

". . . she'll be awfully good with the baby." It was Esther's whisper. "I'm too old to rear a child."

Anna's eyes snapped open and she lay holding her breath, unable to bring the voice into focus. Waiting, she strained to hear more. Was the lady thinking of *giving* her this motherless baby? A tingle of excitement caught between her stomach and her throat.

"And she can cook well for her age. She'll make a good wife for your son."

NO! Her mother and Esther were planning her marriage. To Lesley Horn.

2

Philip's Favorite Subject

*R*ichard Lewis believed that the house belonged to women after sunrise. His raising, he said. "An th' outdoors belongs to a man," he chuckled to Philip Horn. The rusty wire-handled bucket splashed into the windmill's wooden trough that slobbered over with cold, clear water.

"Pretty good reasoning." Philip's eyes went from the overflowing canal to the lean, stringy spokesman. He saw a man as dehydrated as the desert itself. A little more and he would be dried to jerky, Philip thought.

"So you gave up on Californy and you're headed for th' Indian country, huh?" Richard propped one foot upon the gray, weathered tray and spread a leathery hand over his knee.

"Yes, sir. My brother is up there. He's my half brother to be exact, but we always looked out for each other when we were youngsters in knickers. And he still feels kindly toward me. He has been keeping me posted on the land situation. I thought I'd make my fortune in California— or *Esther* thought I would—but most of the good claims on the gold mines were taken up by the time I got there."

"Money has a way of takin' wing."

"You're mighty right. But land can't fly, Mr. Lewis, so I plan to be in on the *start* of this land run they're having in the Indian country. The government is getting ready to give away two million acres of the best land on the face of God's earth. And it's first come, first get it. People will be coming from everywhere, the schemers and the dreamers. But I'm going there to stick and stay."

Richard kicked the bucket with the toe of his worn boot. "I thought the government gave all that Oklahomy land to th' Indians away back, Mr. Horn. If I recollect rightly, President Andrew Jackson promised th' Indians he moved there that their new home would be their very own. Let's see, now. What were his precise words? 'For as long as the grass grows or the water runs, in peace and plenty.' Now wasn't that exactly what he said?"

"He said that all right. And he meant it."

"Then why is the government takin' th' land away from them and breakin' a promise?" Unfairness in man or agency nettled Richard. "If our own government can't be depended on . . ."

"This land is not occupied by the Indians. For a fact, Mr. Lewis, it got left out of the assigning to any Indian tribe back in 1866. The land was neither included in New Mexico when it was organized in '50 nor yet in Kansas four years later. It didn't show up in *any* territory. It was a mistake and one of the Cherokees' own lawyers, Colonel Elias C. Boudinot, first published that mistake.

"I saw the piece myself in the *Chicago Times* the year before I went to California, it was. It interested me, so I tore it out and kept it. The reading said that it could be settled by homesteaders. I sat down and wrote to Mr.

22

Boudinot for more information and got a most courteous answer with a map telling me how to reach the new country and a circular telling all about it.

"I was for going right then, but Esther wouldn't hear to moving to 'that primitive place' as she called it. She pestered me to go to California where things were modern. She said she didn't want to rear our Lesley in 'ignorance and poverty.' I shouldn't have catered to her. I've been miserable, did poorly on the West Coast, and wished for Oklahoma all these years."

"Th' land is just layin' without inhabitant?"

"Yes, sir, and that isn't good for any land. Invites trouble of beast and man. Why, the Ottawa chief, John Earlie, *wants* the territory opened up. Of course, not all the Indians are in agreement with him." Philip scratched at his stubble of scruffy chin whiskers. "Some of them oppose this very much. They want to hold their lands in common like they've always done. Each of the Five Civilized Tribes—the Cherokee, Creek, Seminole, Choctaw, and Chickasaw—sent some men to Washington to oppose the talk of letting the land to settlers. But Bud says the opening is bound to come."

"Th' date for th' openin' hasn't been set?"

"Not yet. They've been tossing it around in Washington for years, but Bud said he thinks it will open up by spring. His reasoning is that they'll let the homesteaders in to make a crop next year. And they say it's going to be like the '49ers stampede to California." He slapped his hamlike hands together. "They can have their gold; I want *land*."

"Seems you could have found some land a mite closer."

23

"All land isn't the same, Mr. Lewis. I want *productive* land. I've always had an eye for that part of the country. It's been a story of rich adventure ever since that Spanish man, Francisco Vasquez de Coronado, went there looking for those Seven Golden Cities."

"Seven Golden Cities?"

"Yes. The Seven Cities of Cibolo. It was told that the people of those cities wore long robes and had dishes of gold and silver."

"Nobody really believed that, did they?"

"For a fact they did. A priest named Fray Marcas . . . oh, but I'm boring you."

"No, no, go on."

"Mr. Marcas said he'd *seen* these wonderful cities from the top of a hill. The viceroy of Mexico sent an army of three hundred horsemen, seventy foot soldiers, and more than a thousand Indians with bows and arrows to conquer the golden towns. Coronado headed up the army himself.

"Well, sir, when they came to the hill, they saw the cities all right. But they were only small adobe villages basking in the sun and occupied by Indians. There was neither gold nor silver—but there were some mad soldiers!"

"Can't blame them."

"You would have thought they had learned their lesson, wouldn't you? But they met up with an old Indian called the Turk. He told them about Quivira. It was *saturated* with gold and silver, he said. This new fable lured the whole army in search of that rich country. After they'd traveled for more than a month, the Indian admitted that he'd told the lie to lead the army away from his people!"

24

"Smart Indian."

"Coronado finally wised up that there were no golden cities. He had been traveling for three years and saw a lot of the Indian country where we're going. He was ready to go home to his beautiful wife. One of his soldiers wrote about the trip and that's how we know about it." Philip stopped to catch his breath. "Really, Mr. Lewis, I'm not much of a talker."

"I don't see how you remember all them details."

"I'm a reader. I learned all I could about the land where I've put my future hopes and ambitions. I can read maps and figure geography. That's simple. But for the life of me, Mr. Lewis, I can't figure *people*. The more I learn of them, the less I seem to know." He threw a cautious look toward the Lewis residence and lowered his voice. "Especially women. Esther has fought me all the way. If pride's a germ, then she's a sick woman. No woman on earth was ever more prideful. What matters if the governor's wife wears wool challis, alpaca, or Henrietta cloth? We didn't bring a thing into the world with us and the death hearse doesn't have a luggage box for us to carry anything to the next world."

Richard shrugged. "Some things ain't worth th' argument. Especially with womenfolks."

"*Some* things. But *land* is. And I don't know if you want to hear the rest of the story about that land . . ."

"Tell on."

"The French came after the Spanish. The Spanish were land men, but the French - they were water men. They came up the rivers in canoes looking for furs. Traders, they were. So that's how it came about that both Spain and France felt like they had a right to call the land theirs."

25

"The first one there had the rights." Richard's sense of righteousness surfaced again.

"Well, it was tossed from one to the other. It makes no matter to me who had it when. What is important is that Napoleon Bonaparte sold it to the United States in the year of 1803. It was all mixed in with Louisiana then. Now wouldn't you call that a brilliant history?"

"I believe you could have been a history tutor, Mr. Horn."

Philip laughed, a full, deep laugh. "You can't recite all day on one subject. And that's what I would be doing. I like men who dream dreams and see visions and have the guts to make their dreams come true. Esther has tried threats, scare tactics, and promises to keep me from making this trip. She said some bad would come of it. She wheedled and cried, but my life is running out, and I want to see at least one dream come true—and that's to have my own land. And not just any land, mind you. I want *Oklahoma* land. I finally just threatened to go without her."

"Your brother is already there?"

"Yes, he's a squatter. He's had some trouble staying, to be sure. He went in with Captain Payne's colony about the time I headed west. One of the 325 original wagons. Mr. Payne was a member of the Kansas legislature and had been working on opening up the land since back in '70. He made many a trip to Washington. Even got himself arrested when he tried to return in '80 over by Bitter Creek, but he never gave up. Nor did Bud. It became almost a game with them, I think. They kept going in and getting put out again.

"Bud was arrested once and taken off to soldier's

26

camp. They sent him across the South Canadian River with orders not to go back into the territory. But he went right back to his place. And the funny thing was, he never did hold any ill-will against those that arrested him. Bud's real good-natured."

"And this Mr. Payne is still trippin' back and forth to Washington?"

"No, he died four years ago. Back in '84. But by then Bud knew his way around the territory pretty well. He knows where the best land is."

"Will you farm there?"

"Farm, ranch, garden. Bud says the land is next door to paradise. The whole countryside is carpeted with knee-high buffalo and blue-stem grass. Virgin land just waiting for the first plow to bite in. Anything will grow. The soil's free of rock, there's no swamps or forests, and there's plenty of good water and all kinds of wildlife for food. And all for free. Can you believe it, Mr. Lewis?"

"Sounds good. Sounds mighty good." Richard gave a heartsick sigh. His weary eyes evaluated the dry, stingy land under his feet. The dread of another scrimpy winter made his jaw muscles tighten when he weighed the productivity of these sun-bleached plains in the balances and found it wanting. "I hope you find your Garden of Eden, Mr. Horn. Seems there's always been the bite of a serpent somewhere in mine."

"They call it the Promised Land. We're going in from the south end. Bud told me just which crossing would be best. He drew me a map of sorts."

"Ain't you goin' awful early, if the openin' isn't till spring?"

"I want to get there before cold weather sets in. We

can winter in our wagon or in a dugout on the borders of the land. Esther isn't going to like it. But I figure whatever inconveniences we have to suffer for a few months won't hold a light to what we stand to gain. She'll understand that later on.

"There's a bit of town about four miles upstream from the crossing. In the Chickasaw Nation. A little place called Purcell. The opinion is that there'll be fewer people crossing there—and it's the pick of the land. Most of the rush will be coming down from the north through Kansas, they're predicting. My brother wants me to claim between the South Canadian River and a place called Oklahoma Station."

Jason came to take the forgotten bucket of water to the livestock. Mr. Horn's talk of a land between the South Canadian River and a place called Oklahoma Station had his father mesmerized. He needed the mental outlet. Without interrupting, Jason moved away.

Philip talked on, intoxicated with his subject. "Each claimant gets 160 free acres. I can claim for me and Esther, and Lesley can claim on his own. Of course, we'll need claims side by side since Esther will be caring for Lesley's child. *If* the child lives the winter out, that is. I hardly think that's likely. The frontier is no place for a motherless infant.

"Esther predicted some bad would come of this trip, and I figured she would blame me for our daughter-in-law's death. But she didn't. I thank God for that. But if the baby dies, too . . ."

A look of pain crossed Richard's chapped face. He rubbed his skinny, bark-brown neck. "I'd say you could leave the baby here until you are settled on your land, but . . ."

28

Philip waited for Richard to go on.

His words snagged on thorns of memory. ". . . I don't believe I could stand to dig one more little grave. We've . . . we've several on the flats yonder now, and the wife is bitter about it. I couldn't pick up the shovel for a—*girl* child." It was a quiet speech, filled with deep hurt.

"I see." Philip's kind eyes offered man-to-man sympathy. "You've been generous enough already, Mr. Lewis. Lodging us the night may have prevented more bad luck for us. If the baby dies, we'll just lay her away wherever she happens to pass on, as we did her mother."

"What kind of travelin' time are you makin'?" Richard slid the talk away from the grievous subject.

"These old plugs I've got don't like to pull the old bone-shaker more than twenty-five miles in one day. And we lose time"—he gave a sawed-off laugh—"in sandstorms. But all in all, we aren't doing badly."

He filled his lungs with a tonic breath of light, crisp air. "What's so amazing about this place, Mr. Lewis, is that one would never guess this morning that there was such a storm yesterday!"

3
The Pawn

I *didn't hear it! I didn't! It can't be so!* Anna's head throbbed with the pressure of racing blood. Waves of hot anger and cold fear crashed in upon her reeling mind. *Esther Horn is planning my marriage to her son, and my mother is in agreement!*

A thousand thronging sensations came and went. Betrayal. Despair. Incredulity. Dread. Confusion. How could one's own parent become a cruel turncoat, undermining her daughter's future happiness? She gritted her teeth to stop their nervous chattering.

Had everyone, everything turned traitor? Even the plains that had been her lifetime home seemed to mock her, to play Judas. If she lived in a wooded area, she told herself, she could hide in the forest until the awful man was gone. Any other land would befriend her, help her esape. But how could she hope to find seclusion behind the spindly leg of a windmill?

Her mind darted from one dead-end road to another. If she dared try to run away on this flat, naked expanse of nothingness, she might wander for miles without finding habitation or food. How far was it to Lubbock? To

Lamesa? To Tahoka? She knew only the general direction of these places. Indeed, with so little knowledge of her surroundings, she would surely roam to her death. But that fear was eclipsed by a worse one: she would be discovered and hauled back to marry Lesley.

"Lesley needs a wife," Esther Horn talked on. "Any man that has a child needs a woman. Once a man has left the family home and married, it's never the same for him back with his parents. He is out of place in both worlds, if you know what I mean. He doesn't fit with the married or with the unmarried. "You can see for yourself how your son and mine aren't comrades. That's a good example of what I'm talking about. Some folks don't think it's respectful to marry again right away, but most agree that having a helpless child makes an exception to the rule. Wouldn't you think so?"

"Yes, I'd think so."

"I saw Lesley looking at your daughter when we came in last evening. He was taking stock of her. I saw it in his eyes. I read Lesley pretty well. I'd say by what I saw that he wouldn't object to the idea of marrying her. She's about the size and shape of his wife that died, only she's even more fetching of face. Looks shouldn't matter to a man, but Lesley does have a penchant for pretty faces."

"Anna's not afraid of hard work," encouraged Corine. The eager, clipped words rolled from her tongue. "I've trained her well. Besides cookin', she can knit and darn and cross-stitch. Now she ain't had no baby experience . . ."

"No worries. Tending babies comes natural with girls. She kept the sick one from crying the night, didn't she? That's more than *I've* been able to do. We really don't expect the child to live anyhow, and by the time she gets her own to tend . . ."

Anna pushed back a rush of nausea. So this disgraceful conspiracy was the payment she got for doing a good turn! Sold! Bartered off to a worthless man! *Whatever you do, don't let Maw pawn you off to the first rat that comes along.* Jason's words echoed back. The chess game had begun, and Corine Lewis had her hand on the pawn, soon to be captured by Esther Horn and her soul-scarred son. And what move could Anna make to block the capture? With such powerful opponents, escape seemed hopeless.

"Anna has always been an odd, quiet thing."

"That's no problem. Lesley's first wife was the same way," cut in Esther. "He likes to dominate in a conversation anyhow, and a woman is a woman to him."

"She ain't never had a beau an' she might shy off if we mention marriage to her. Then again, she might jump at the chance to be a bride. Livin' out here on th' plains like we do, she ain't had no one to spark. My son wanted to take her into town, but you can't tell what wild devilment might get into a girl that's been cooped up for seventeen years. Mayhap I just don't trust her. Richard allows I don't even *understand* her. But I think it would be better—and safer—to see her married off to some nice young man like your son. Like I told Richard, no girl should be a weight to her family after age eighteen if she has a chance to wed properlike."

"When will your girl turn eighteen?"

Eyes upward, Corine counted on her fingers. "In four months, two weeks, and three days. I recall well th' day of her birth. It was three days after—"She bit the sentence in half.

33

"Three days after what, Mrs. Lewis?"

"Nuthin'. It wouldn't make no matter to you nohow."

"Well, it sounds planned in heaven, doesn't it? She'll already be eighteen by the time we get to our land."

"Your land?"

"We're on our way to the territory of Oklahoma to get us some free land. Every family gets 160 acres. Lesley probably wouldn't want to marry your daughter before we get there and knock himself out of the extra 160 acres that she could get."

"Anna can get free land, too?"

"Yes. The Unassigned Lands Law specifies that single women, widows, and divorced lady folks are eligible for the same amount of land as a man under the Homestead Act."

Corine nodded, but her blank look left reason to doubt her comprehension of Esther's great store of worldly wisdom.

The simmering of the teakettle filled in a silence created by the two plotting women busy setting bread at the stove. The high, hissing sound matched Anna's runaway emotions; her heart throbbed like a muffled drum. Should she scream out her objections, letting them know she had heard all their diabolical scheming?

Esther started to talk again, and Anna felt it necessary to hear all that was said so that she might be forearmed.

"If you have no objections, Mrs. Lewis, we'll take your daughter along with us. As a nursemaid for the baby, we'll tell her. By the time we reach the territory, she will be madly in love with Lesley. Lesley has a way with ladyfolks." Accustomed to arranging other people's affairs,

Esther wasted no time in the planning of Lesley's future. Her philosophy was that people, like sheep, must be firmly guided lest they stray. And her son would stray without a tether.

"I'll have to talk to my husband about letting Anna go," Corine said. "It'll be one less mouth to feed here—and things are tight right now. He'll put up a squawk, but ever'body knows that daughters are for growin' up an' gettin' married off. He expected it right from th' start. I'll remind him that *I* was younger than Anna when we married."

"I don't know about raising girls," Esther sighed. "I only had the one boy, and Philip declares I spoiled him. He does tend to be a bit wild, but he'll settle down with time and age. Human nature is fickle when it's young, my father always said. Even the good Lord said let the tares grow up with the wheat. I always allowed that meant the good and the bad in our lives. Like I told Philip, all of us have evil habits and good habits. But if we try to pluck the bad habits out all at once, we might destroy some of the good things in life along with the bad. That makes sense, doesn't it?" She didn't wait for Corine to answer. "So I don't worry about a few tares."

Corine drew her brows together in a brown study. "But I'm not sure Richard will want to let Anna go with pure strangers."

"Oh, I hope you don't feel like we are strangers, Mrs. Lewis! Anna would be marrying well. She could certainly hope to do no better for herself. Who but a law-dodging drifter would ever come to stay in this desolate place?"

"I didn't mean . . ."

"We're an upstanding family from a good bloodline.

We haven't any nervous skeletons in the closet trying to hide and afraid of being caught. We're natives of Louisiana, and as I told you when we came, we've been out to California for the past eight years. We went out around the turn of the '80's for the gold. I thought Lesley could get a better education out there, too. The schoolmasters were better paid on the West Coast. Better taught by the better bought, I always said. Lesley—a typical, mischievous boy—was often truant and troublesome to his instructors, but he finally got a fair education."

"Seems you would want to stay in Californy where things was goin' good."

"Actually, the big gold rush had petered out by the time we got there. Philip takes so long making up his mind to do a thing that the good opportunities are past when he finally gets a move on. Now if he had gone when I first set in on him, we'd be wealthy."

"Men can be balky."

"There's never been a balkier man than Philip Horn, Mrs. Lewis." Esther's laugh—if that was what it was meant to be—was a failure. She resumed her subject, "When I saw we could make *scarcely* more than a hand-to-mouth living in that tough brawly state, I *insisted* on us going somewhere else."

Corine's eyes examined Esther's expensive dress, which was many steps up the social ladder from her own ragged yarn-dyed garment. She said nothing.

"About that time," Esther talked on, "we got word from Philip's brother about the Boomer movement in the Oklahoma Territory. He wrote us all about it. He says there are millions of acres of that skillet-shaped land to be let for the taking. And it's not *charity,* Mrs. Lewis.

Those of us who are going are doing the government a *favor* by cultivating the land."

"Philip wants to be there when the bugle sounds. He says gold comes and goes, but land is forever. And he's right about that. I can hardly wait to get there! Do you think your husband would be interested in some of the land?"

"Oh, we . . . couldn't leave our home here." The lame words hobbled out, held up by crutches of bitterness. "I've . . . memories here I couldn't . . . move away from."

"Philip wanted to go up there years ago, but I thought we should wait until the president said we could go in. The wonderful land was surveyed and marked by the Barrett Survey away back in 1873, but the government has held back on giving it out. I thought it would only be fair to wait. Then Philip's brother wrote that we should come on.

"He has scouted out the best land there. Why, he said if he could own heaven and the territory both, he'd lease out heaven and live in the territory." She chuckled. "Excuse his loose mouth, Mrs. Lewis. That sounds like something Philip's brother would say. That's where Lesley gets his loose mouth—from Philip's side of the family."

Corine listened with a sort of hero worship. Esther's attempts to prove her superiority and establish herself as a worthy mother-in-law for Anna were a success. However, Corine's dark eyes still clouded and cleared. Esther worried when they clouded and relaxed when they cleared, watching closely. Now they clouded again.

"What's wrong. Mrs. Lewis?"

"Would Anna be in any danger? Richard will want to know that in particular."

"From outlaws? The elements? Wild beasts?"

"No. *Indians.*"

"My dear lady! The territory of Oklahoma doesn't have problems with savages. It's a *tame*land! Don't you remember that the five civilized tribes of Indians signed treaties of alliance with the Confederate States back in 1861? The Indians no longer roam about with their poison arrows. They live on *reservations.* Why, the Choctaws even raised money to send to the Irish famine sufferers. So you see, they're not only civilized themselves, but they are willing to help the rest of the world, too."

"If Richard asks, I'll tell him."

"Oklahoma is so modern that a railroad runs through. The Santa Fe Line. They put that in a year ago. You can't get much more modern than that. Philip sees this new land as an opportunity for a new beginning. And I can tell you, I'm excited!"

Philip Horn would have been astonished to hear Esther's defense of the "primitive land" she claimed to detest. But Esther, thinking only to win a bride for her irascible son, plunged on, gilding her picture with fanciful invention.

"Some allow that the land will open by spring. And some say it'll be the world's biggest horse race."

"Horse race?"

"Philip's brother says they'll just line everybody up at the border and give the signal, and then it's catch as catch can! Won't that be fun, though? Philip wants in on that, come the plagues of Egypt! And if your daughter is with us"—she caught herself—"*since* your daughter will be with us, Lesley can get *twice* as much land. His 160 acres *and* hers. Then, if they wish, they can sell her acreage after they are married and get money to build their home." It was evident that Esther had details worked out far in advance. "Philip says we aren't getting any younger, and he wants to get somewhere and settle down on his own property. He says he feels like these weeds you have here. What do you call them?"

"Tumbleweeds?"

"That's it. Tumbleweeds. Your knowledge of the prairie is remarkable, Mrs. Lewis."

Corine beamed.

"I'm not superstitious and I'm not much on believing in luck or destiny, but if that awful sandstorm gets Lesley a new wife, I can say it was a blessing."

Jason stepped through the front door with a pail of fresh drinking water for his mother. The last phrase of Esther's sentence stopped him granite still. He looked from Corine to Esther and back again. Esther didn't flinch, but Corine tucked her head with guilt.

"Who was she talking about, Maw?"

The paralyzed stillness seemed to demand a whispered answer. "Her son."

"The one with them?"

"That's their one an' only son."

"She's not talking about *Anna* marrying him, is she?"

Corine faltered beneath his steely glare. "Why . . . yes, I think mayhap she probably might be."

"Anna isn't ready for marriage, Maw."

"You don't know nuthin' about girls, Jason. Lots of girls get married younger than Anna. I did. These people are from good raisin', and Anna couldn't do no better for herself."

"Does Anna . . . ?"

39

"The Horns plan on takin' her with them up to Oklahomy, and she'll marry after she's birthdayed and gets her some land of her own—unless she don't want to wait that long to wed." Her frosty words sent chills up Jason's shoulders. He turned and left abruptly, his face contorted with anger.

Jason! Anna heard his remonstration. He would help her! He would surely find a way to block her capture. Her brother, her knight! He would put a chess piece between her and her antagonist. Esther could not get her. She found comfort in the thought.

But as soon as the winged thought was born, it died. Her mother would take great care that she have no opportunity to speak with her brother. Her mother wished her married.

Jason's few words of protest revealed that he was against his mother's plan. And now she would be wary.

4

Inner Storm

*T*he baby's outcry of hunger hushed the talk and stopped the shuffling feet beyond Anna's sequestered sleeping quarters.

"I'm afraid your daughter and the baby are waking," whispered Esther.

Anna expected the grandmother to relieve her of the child's care and prepare its food. But she did not. Her actions said that Lesley's child belonged to the future wife now, and the sooner she learned to meet its demands the better.

She moved past the muted women to the kitchen stove. Holding the whimpering infant in one arm, she prepared the bottle with her free hand. Her seething wrath bolstered her determination not to ask for help from the insensitive Esther. She kept her swollen eyes carefully averted, afraid that her intense disgust for the deceit of both women might show in them.

Esther's unbroken gaze reached out like a net and caught her. "You're so good with the baby," she said. "I slept the whole night through. I didn't wake up once!"

"Yes, Anna, you're so handy with the baby that Mrs.

Horn has mentioned offering you a job as nursemaid."

"I'm quite selective about my employees. But you have the qualifications."

"Of course, you would be obliged to travel with them, Anna. But I'm sure you would like that. You've always wanted to go into town with Jason." Her mother's words hit like a slap.

Anna smiled, a smile assumed at such a cost that she felt her face would crack. "I have plenty to do here, thank you, Mrs. Horn. I wouldn't care for the nursemaid job that you offer."

"You don't know what you are turning down, young lady."

"I think I do."

"And anyway, I need you. Your mother assures me that she can spare you. I'm not physically able to care for a child so small and sickly. I've been puny for the last few years. I need to be getting care instead of giving it. And the baby needs a younger and stronger nurse if she is to survive."

"I have . . . other plans."

"Why, Anna, we have no plans. And if we did, they could be changed out here on this bald prairie. You mustn't be rude. I've taught you better. Mrs. Horn has said that she had need of you. You'll go right along with her to help her, of course! I can manage this tiny house with Willy to run my errands."

"We're going to the Oklahoma Territory, my dear girl. It's a *beautiful* land." Esther talked faster and faster. "There's plenty of free acreage, and you'll be well cared for. We can't pay you in money, but you'll get your hire. It's a golden opportunity any young lady would envy.

Why, you might even have a chance to meet and marry a rich landowner there. That's more than you can hope for here in this forsaken place, I'm afraid."

"I don't wish to marry, thank you."

"All girls wish to marry," corrected Esther, as if Anna had no reasoning power of her own. "I was your age once, and I *know*."

"I'm sure Anna *does* wish to marry, Mrs. Horn. She's just a wee bit shy—and you are a stranger to her," Corine said. "She'll get warmer and less edgy with time."

"Oh, I understand," Esther's child-placating tone vexed Anna. "We'll get acquainted. We'll have miles and miles to get to know each other quite well—and for Anna to get to know *all* my family."

"When I'm ready for a husband, my brother Jason will help me find a good, honest man. He said I needn't take the first rat that came across the desert."

"You will not be impudent, Anna!" Her mother's tone took her to task. Anna could never remember such a rebuke, and she lowered her eyes in humiliation. "You may go and pack your things. Take all that's yours, but don't take anything that ain't."

"No, Maw, I . . ."

"There's a towsack under th' washstand that'll suffice for a portmanteau. Mr. Horn wishes to be to th' territory ahead of th' cold weather and won't want to be delayed by waitin' on you to dally."

"Please, Maw . . ." The protest that trembled on Anna's lips met with unbending resistance.

"Here." Esther held out her arms. "Let me have the baby long enough for you to get your clothes together. You'll have plenty of time to hold her on the trip."

Anna stood rooted to the sandy floor. Last evening's searing sandstorm could not compare to the storm that raged in her heart. She wanted nothing to do with Lesley Horn! A mad blizzard of raging anger mingled with bitter resentment while cacti of piercing fear mutilated all hope that had ever lived in her young body. But in this fury, the gritty feeling wasn't on her teeth, nor was the abrasion on her feet. It was on her soul. As she stood there like a petrified rock, she felt her breath being smothered off by the violence of the storm. Would it ever end?

"I'll pack her things for her, Mrs. Horn." Corine Lewis moved away, ignoring Anna's stance of resistance and the desperate plea in her eyes. "She won't burden you with much baggage."

"Lesley will be glad to load her belongings when you get them ready. I'll likely have to go wake him. That boy! I believe he could spend his life in sleeping. But it's the grief, of course. Some can't sleep, and others sleep too much."

"Where is your son?" ventured Corine.

"Sometime this morning, he slipped out of the house and to the wagon. I guess he's there yet. Most of his mourning is spent there. Lesley keeps a jug of spirits hidden from his father. If Philip knew it, he would be furious. Philip's a teetotaler. But what is a poor boy to do to help his sore heart? I say the drink is just medicine for his tormented mind! When he gets mar—" her hand flew up to cover her mouth as Corine cleared her throat in a gesture of warning. "He'll put away his medicine when his heart is healed," she finished. "And that won't be long."

"Of course," agreed Corine.

Inside, Anna felt bankrupt and empty with no resources left to draw from. She'd been captured, like a soul-less animal. "When . . . will we . . . leave?" She choked on the stunted sentence.

"First thing in the morning. Philip wants to start with dayburst. I'm surprised he's stayed the day, but he seems to have found a friend in your father."

Jason! Oh, Jason! I must talk to you! Anna watched and waited, but the day passed and night came and her brother had not returned.

5

Convincing Richard

"Did ya hear me, Richard Lewis?" Corine sat upright on her pallet and used her archless brown foot to gouge her sleeping husband.

"Huh?"

"I said Jason ain't in yet. And I won't sleep until you go out and find him."

"Jason's no child. He'll come in when he's good and ready." Richard's voice was thick with drowsiness.

"He ain't never been this late before."

"Uh-huh."

"You ain't listenin', Richard. I said . . ."

"Jason's been upset all day. Cut the boy some slack. He's man-aged now and you still treat him like a juvenile."

"I don't think he likes Lesley Horn."

"Lesley smacks of laziness. Jason can't abide a man with more dirt on his tongue than on his hands."

"It ain't laziness. It's pure grief. Mrs. Horn told me plain that he ain't never got over his sorrowin' for his young wife that passed on just a few days yon. He's got a big, lovin' heart. That's why he's hurtin' so."

"Big, lovin' hearts don't harness up with meanness."

47

"What do you mean by that?"

"Jason caught him mistreatin' one of the animals. There's no excuse for cruelty, Corine. However he's hur- tin', he shouldn't lash out to hurt somethin' else. Anybody that would be mean to a helpless animal would slight a human, too."

"Pshaw! Jason's idea of mistreatin' animals is to look at them cross-eyed! You know yourself that Jason has spoilt our team by not bein' firm enough with them. They need a correctin' hand."

"I didn't say it was *our* animal."

"Well, I reckon-so he has a right to do what he will with his own livestock."

"I reckon-so he hasn't a right to beat and kick a horse. *Any* horse!"

"His maw says he'll not get over his lonesomeness until he finds another wife to take that one's place."

"The dead wife is scarcely cold yet, Corine. I should think neither he *nor* his mother would be thinking on a replacement just yet. I don't like the idea of a man lookin' for a woman just for a nursemaid and a slave. I hope there's still such a thing as real love."

Snores rumbled from the Horns' corner. "A little quieter, Richard! Lesley might hear you."

"There's no danger. He's nightin' in the wagon."

"Poor thing. You wouldn't know grief if you met it face on."

"No? I've met heartbreak five times when five of my sons took to the earth. Not many things can be more cut- tin' to a heart than layin' away your hopes for th' future."

"Shhh. Not so loud! There's but a curtain atwixt us and th' sleepers. We don't want to wake them. They have

48

a long day of travel ahead of them tomorrow."

"Mayhap after they leave Jason will lay down his grouch."

"Have you thought that Jason's upset might be because someone his age showed up that is more handsome? I seen challenge in his eyes."

"Lesley Horn? More handsome than our Jason? With his short-legged build and mouse-colored hair? My lady, your eyesight is failin' worse than I thought. Lesley's shifty eyes can't fetch a light to Jason's clear ones. I can hardly abide our young guest myself, now that he's made himself a pain all day with his foul moods. He's . . . cocky."

"Why, I think he's quite mannerly, Richard. Jason hasn't given him a fair chance."

"I'll just be glad when Jason doesn't have to put up with the young man's impudence any more."

Corine gave a thin cough, a giveaway sign of her approach to a touchy proposition. "Their leavin' brings to mind a question."

"Yes?"

"What would you think of us lettin' Anna go on this trip with th' Horns to help out with th' sick child? Mrs. Horn offered her a good payin' job."

"This isn't Lesley's scheming, is it?"

"Lesley never once mentioned it."

Richard sucked in his breath. Corine lay holding hers. "This ain't got nuthin' to do with Lesley Horn's woman hunt, does it?"

Corine hedged. "Esther needs a nurse for th' infant, Richard. She's not a bit well, and th' care of th' child is makin' her weaker."

"Does Anna *want* to go and work for Mrs. Horn?"

49

"Well, she didn't really say one way or t'other as I recollect. But I was thinkin' what a good chance it would be for her to see more of life than bein' stuck here with no one to feather with. It would be a good experience for her, too. And with things so skimpy here. . ."

"I'll make a livin' for us all somehow, Corine. I don't plan to send a girl out in the world to forage for herself. I'm an able-bodied man and she's part of my family obligation."

"I can tell you it's an envious opportunity that Mrs. Horn is offerin' her. I can't believe you'd stand in her way of betterin' herself and makin' progress. She could even get her some land."

"If she's really wishin' to go, I wouldn't stand in her path. What would be her wages?"

"That would be fixed between her and Mrs. Horn. Mrs. Horn did say she'd be paid well, though, after they reach th' territory. I told Mrs. Horn I didn't expect you'd object—put in those terms."

"How long will the job last? And will they see that Anna is returned home safe to us when she's finished th' task? You have to think of these things from every angle."

"That would depend."

"Depend on what?"

"Why, Richard, bein' nigh on to eighteen, th' girl might up and meet someone on th' trip or in th' territory and fall in love and marry!"

"I wouldn't find no fault with that so long as it was her own free choice. She's perceptive and a good judge of people. I'd trust her decision in choosin' a man."

"Who else's choice would it be but her own?"

"I would want to know no one put any pressure on her."

"I ain't never seen a bigger worry-wart than you, Richard. I've thought it over from front to back, and I think it'd be best for our Anna to go along with them. Good fortune don't come knockin' at life's door often."

"It's so . . . sudden. I find it regrettish that Anna wants to leave home. I had some plans for her. I always wanted us to take her back, and show her the old home-place where she was born. . ."

"Anna ain't a bit interested in history. The *now* livin' is what's important to this young generation. They ain't sentimental like old folks."

"Well, I knew in my heart that we'd not be keepin' her around for always. If she really wants to go, I won't try to talk her out of it. The choice is hers."

"I'd rather you not talk to her about it at all. If she gets th' notion that you'll be missin' her or regrettin' her takin' th' employment, she'll forget about what *she* wants and try to please *you*."

"Does Jason and Willy know about her decisions?"

"Willy don't. But he won't give a care. As long as he's got his fleabitten cat and a hen or a lizard, he's got friends enough. If he misses her at all, it'll be a short miss."

"Does Jason know?"

"Well . . . sort of, I suspect."

"Sort of?"

"He walked in while Mrs. Horn and me was talkin' about . . . about it."

"And it galled him?"

"Can't you see, Richard Horn, that the time has come for Anna to live her own life? Jason humors the girl. He'll be wantin' to take her into town with him afore long, and

I won't have it!''

"Corine! Jason only wants th' best for Anna, as any young man would want for a younger sister!"

Neither of them heard Jason come in. Nor would they ever know how deeply the acid words he heard burned into his soul.

6
The Leaving

"I trust that you will take good care of my daughter, Mr. Horn." Richard helped Philip hitch up the team.

"I'll do my best, Mr. Lewis."

"I'm findin' it hard to let her go so far from home. But th' wife says she wants to go. And I wouldn't want to be guilty of discouragin' her from a wise decision. It just ain't . . . like her. She's been such a homebody. Never once mentioned wantin' to go away until now. She's nigh growed up, though, and I guess every young lady wants to try her own wings at some time or other. She's a good and dependable girl. Never gave us a breath's trouble nor backtalk in her life. She won't give you any, either."

"Esther is relieved that the girl wishes to go along and help with the baby. And I can't tell you how I appreciate it, Mr. Lewis. Since the girl made up her mind to go along with us, my wife has been a different person. Why, she even seems *excited* about going to the territory now! I guess it *was* hard to travel with no one of her kind to talk to. Women live in worlds of their own—and have their own problems. Esther's been poorly for some time now, and the care of the child drags her down. She's never been handy with babies. I hope we can repay you in some way for your kindness. I guess the good Lord just sent that sandstorm to bring this good fortune to us."

Philip, trusting of nature, seldom saw past the surface of Esther's devious designs. He had taken them at face value for all their wedded years, wondering at the strange coincidences that always culminated to her liking. He rarely questioned her methods, never delving for hidden motives. That his son, Lesley, figured into the tangled plot of employing Anna as nursemaid did not cross his mind.

"You'll see that Anna gets home in the event the baby . . . goes, won't you?"

"We couldn't very well turn around and bring her back if we're nearer the territory than we are here. It would cause delay and expense. You understand that we couldn't forfeit our land for her."

"Of course."

"But we would get her back as soon as we could."

"That's all I would ask."

"She'll be able to get her own land."

"My wife mentioned that."

"It would be worth her while to go on with us—even if the child dies—just for the land. For that matter, if she gets homesick, she has but to sell her land and pay her fare home to you with money to spare. This trip could prove profitable to all of you."

Philip's lack of duplicity eased Richard's apprehension. He recognized in Mr. Horn an honest man, a man to be trusted. "My prayers follow you," he promised. "And my Anna."

54

"There's plenty of land for everyone. I think you should think about joining us. I'd like to be neighbored by a man like you. You'd get away from these sand-storms." Philip grinned. "And there's enough moisture in the territory to grow more than one prickly-pear patch."

A wearied expression made Richard seem older than his half century. "Sometimes I think it would be best to leave memories behind and start all over anew." He shook his head as if to clear away past haunts. "Anna has prob-ably made a smart choice. Who knows? Maybe she'll find happiness in your new country. How the girl deserves it!"

Philip shifted his weight from one foot to the other. "Your daughter will have a piece of choice land if you decide to relocate. Who knows what the future holds?"

Richard shrugged. "Sometimes I wish I knew. At other times, I'm glad I don't."

Philip cleared his throat with a need to speak his con-science. "I wouldn't want to leave without being square with you, Mr. Lewis. Where we're taking your daughter is not a place known for its tameness. I don't think any harm will befall us, but a man certainly wouldn't want to go without his Winchester. It's a country without much law and order, I'm afraid."

"My daughter was born in a lawless part of th' coun-try, sir. Wherever we be, there's a certain risk that makes us dependent on our Maker for protection."

"My brother said that in one year there were over 365 murders. That's averaging one a day. And that's a lot of people to die of lead poisoning. That's mostly men, though."

"What about th' ladyfolks? Are they in particular dan-ger?"

"Oh, no. Bud has met many of the outlaws in person. He says most of them are *good* bad men, if that makes any sense. They won't harm ladyfolks or children—and they make it mighty unpleasant for those who do."

"That's more than I could say for Anna's birthplace. Women and children made no matter to th' heathen there. But she remembers nothin' of th' violence, and we haven't told her. It ain't a pretty history. We came here when she was scarce two year old to escape th' injustices of that area."

"I see."

"Remember, she's a tender one. She don't know nuthin' about swindlers or pickpockets or confidence men that swarm them frontier boom towns. She hasn't been off th' place here. I'd just ask you to look to her welfare like you would if she was your own flesh and blood."

Philip shot his hand out for a pledging shake as the passengers that would occupy the wagon came out of the house for boarding. The luggage had already been loaded, and only the goodbyes were unfinished.

Anna, holding the child, refused to lift her head. The tears played too near the surface of her smarting eyes. They would run loose without diligent restraint.

Lesley jumped into the schooner and reached out pretentious arms to help her into the vehicle.

"What a gentleman!" Corine cooed. "See, Anna, Lesley will help you up." Anna recoiled from her mother's hypocritical pat.

With an artful movement, Anna handed the blanketed child up to Lesley's waiting arms. He flushed in confusion. Then she turned imploring eyes upon her father. "Will you help me up, Paw?"

As Richard put his hands about her thin waist to hoist her, she pushed back with all her strength. She couldn't bring herself to get in the wagon with Lesley Horn. Her whole body trembled, and the dam that held back the tears crumbled.

"What is it, Anna?"

"Oh, Paw . . . I *can't* go!"

"Of course you can go!" Corine flew to Richard's side to quench any rebellion on the girl's part.

"Quiet, Corine." Richard lifted Anna's stricken face with a gentle hand. "Look at me, Anna. Do you not *want* to go with the Horns?"

All eyes turned on the pale girl. "Oh, no, please, Paw!"

He focused accusing eyes on Corine. "You said . . ."

"It's just the moment of partin', Richard. She'll do fine when she's on her way. We settled this yesterday when Anna packed her clothes."

"But if Anna doesn't want to go, she *shain't!*" Richard's vehement outburst brought courage to Anna, dismay to Corine.

"Now, Mr. Lewis," intercepted Esther in an even mediator monotone, "it's not that your daughter doesn't *want* to go along with us, to be sure. She's a good nursemaid and she wishes to work for me. It's just that she fears *you* are not in entire agreement with her leaving and she is hesitating on your account. It would be most selfish and inconsiderate of you to deny her the ambition to be independent, have her own land, and see new country." She caught Anna's arm, exerting more pressure than could be detected by observation. "Come, dear," she said with a cat sort of smile, "we can't cause Philip any further delay."

Corine's eager push and Esther's firm pull landed Anna's resisting body in the wagon while Richard stood by in a perplexed stupor.

"For pity's sake, Richard, don't make the girl's departure miserable by your own silly sentiments!" There was open scorn in Corine's voice.

"Where is Jason, Corine?" he asked, stalling for time, hoping his delinquent mind could sort out the discrepancy. "He'll surely want to bid his sister farewell. Wait, and I'll go in search of him." He turned to leave.

But Esther urged her husband on like a madwoman. "She's all in, Philip, and we're ready for travel. The hour is growing late. Now let's go!"

Philip slapped the reins across the broad, bronze backs of the team, and they set off at a spanking pace for the Oklahoma Territory with their unwilling guest.

Where was Jason? Anna, her heart sandwiched between the sting of betrayal and a brave sense of loyalty to her brother, felt herself crushed with the unanswered questions that begged answers. Why had he not been there to see her off? He had heard Esther and Corine's plotting—and he knew why Corine sent her away with the Horn family. Was the knowledge that his sister was sold to "a rat" so painful that he could not bear to witness the departure? It couldn't possibly be more painful for him than for her! And her brother was certainly no coward.

All the world had abandoned her. Yet her mind could not accept Jason's final abandonment, too. That concession would be too much to bear—the fatal wound to her broken spirit.

She had had no opportunity to talk with him. Did he

understand that she was going against her will? Oh, surely he did! Questions outran answers as the wheels of the wagon squeaked away from home and safety.

Anna's shoulders slumped in hopelessness. "Forgive me, God," she cried in her grief-pocked heart. "Forgive me for hating the plains . . . the sandstorms. Better a thousand sandstorms than the storm I now face!"

7

Jason's Gift

*A*nna sat in the back of the wagon too stunned with the turn of events for rational thought. In the backward outlook, the adobe house became a speck on the horizon and then lost its outline in the shimmering haze. Her unfocused gaze saw only the endless stretch of prairie riddled with prairiedog holes and silvered with faraway mirages. Had her last peaceful moment been three days—or an eternity—ago?

"If you aren't comfortable in the back of the wagon, you might move up to the front near Lesley and Philip," Esther suggested. "It's less bumpy up there."

"I'm fine, thank you." If words could be starched, these were.

She turned her face toward the rear of the conveyance again and tried to concentrate on the hundreds of jack rabbits that nibbled on the sparse grasses, sitting at a safe distance with ears cocked as the wagon lumbered past. One fearless jack, almost as big as a dog, refused to move, and the horses kicked sand over it as they trotted by. Lizards skittered away from the path of the wheels that had now settled into a slow, steady rhythm.

The vermilion and magenta blossoms of the cactus plants lay open to the power of the September heat. They'd endured the dry summer and never wilted.

Directly above, the sun went into hiding. It seemed to her that the heavenly orb retreated behind a veil of thin clouds with peculiar reluctance on her account; it covered its face just for her. An ironic conceit on her part, perhaps, but as the wagon bumped along, she embraced the strange notion and it brought her a degree of comfort.

The brown burlap bag beside her bulged with her assortment of earthly possessions. She wasn't sure what all her mother had included, so she pulled open the top to have a look. Haphazardly folded threadbare clothing, a thin blanket, a battered doll that Jason had whittled for her from mesquite wood for Christmas, and a faded slat bonnet were all she could see. She was especially glad for the doll and marveled that Corine had been generous enough to include it in the motley lot.

She shut her eyes to remember the place she was leaving because she reasoned that she would probably never return. Her mind filled with joys and hurts. She would miss it all, of course: the hard cot of a bed, the black iron cookstove, the splintery washstand weathered to a sickly gray. But things didn't matter. What she would miss most was her family. Particularly Jason. The thought of never seeing him again set her lips in a thin line of pain.

Lesley had been sullenly mute since their departure from the stucco hut an hour ago. His unpredictable disposition and wide mood swings lowered Anna's evaluation of his character yet further. These, though, were the lesser of the qualities she disliked in the man. He suffered a spiritual disease she could not diagnose, and she deter-

mined to keep her distance from him. She met his possessive glances with repulsion.

A silent strain hung in the air. The only one who
smiled was Esther; she smiled a victor's smile. Her
gloating smirk clearly said she had trapped her victim,
and her prize brought her a thrill of triumph. Now to get
the trophy into her son's hands . . .

The baby lay sleeping on a small, lumpy mattress, her
tiny face twisted into a pinched frown as if a bad dream
tormented her. What was her future? Would not a premature grave be preferable to a living death with a heart-
less father?

While Anna sifted through her confusing emotions,
a cloud of dust mushroomed on the horizon. At first but
a speck, a horse and rider took shape as man and beast
gained distance.

Anna paid the drama scant attention until the man
on horseback became recognizable. It was Jason.

Her heart leaped up in a crazy pattern of hope. Had
her mother changed her mind about sending her away?
Had Jason been sent to fetch her home? Had her father
sent him, perhaps, in response to her final plea? Would
she escape a marriage to the evil-humored man she found
so unbearable? Light flooded the dark places of her mind.
She took the straw of hope and began to build a dream
with no foundation to undergird it.

Seeing her flushed face framed in the oval opening,
Jason motioned to her. She caught up her skirts and hurl-
ed herself over the tailgate of the slow-snaking wagon
and ran toward him in fevered haste. Her wide eyes with
their dark lashes that swept to copper-hued tips registered
such trust that Jason squeezed the saddle horn and turn-

ed his sun-bronzed face away.

"You've come for me, Jason!" she cried with a child-like confidence.

"How I wish I had!" Anguish filled his hollow eyes. "But I have no place to take you . . . just now. If only I had a job in town!" He talked fast, making every moment count. "I'm sorry I was not there to see you off. I slipped in the house to get this for you. Here." He handed her the family Bible. "I knew I'd have to get it while Maw was out of the house. I will be in trouble when she finds it gone. She won't miss it for a long time—until another one is born or someone dies. As the oldest, it's part of my legacy, and I want you to have it. You will need its . . . comfort."

"Thank you, Jason." The words tried to stick in the back of her throat. "I knew there was a reason you were not there to say goodbye. And I wanted to tell you that I don't . . . want to go away."

"I know." His words hid low. "Anna, don't marry that . . . that beast with a deformed soul! They can't make you!"

"Pray for me, Jason."

"Post me a letter to Lubbock, General Delivery. That way Maw won't get it." The words seemed to burst from his chest. He gestured toward the wagon. "Here they come back for you." He pressed a silver dollar into her hand, kissed her cheek, then swung into the saddle. The spurred mount reared and was gone.

Anna stood like a marble statuette, unable to move, looking after her brother. She wanted to run after him, to beg him to take her home with him.

The Horn wagon had ground to a halt and was turning back. Esther yelled to Lesley and Lesley to his father. "She's jumped from the wagon. Stop! Stop! We can't let her!"

"Why, Esther, you act as if she is a fleeing criminal," scolded Philip. "She's forgotten something and her brother has brought whatever it might be. Please calm yourself down or you'll have a stroke."

"But the way she jumped out all of a sudden, Philip, I thought . . ." her words trailed off.

Anna moved slowly toward the wagon. Clutching the Bible to her breast, she looked up to heaven in a prayer of unspoken thanks. A breeze from the east began tearing the clouds apart above her and scattering them, letting the sun smile through. Nothing changed on the outside, but something changed within her. She had the Bible, Jason's legacy. And the Bible represented God.

Esther plunged from the wagon, stumbled, and almost fell. "Why, I was afraid . . ." she began, red-faced. "I mean, did your mother send something that you had forgotten?"

"My brother brought me the family Bible and a dollar."

"Of course. How nice of your mother to remember those little details. Money is always useful, and you'll need the Bible to record your marriage to Lesley and the births of your children in the new territory. Did you know that such records will hold up in court after a certain number of years? I'm sure your mother has your birth properly recorded. You might have to show proof of your age when you register for your land. You've a prudent mother, Anna. On first evaluation one wouldn't give her credit for such forethought.

65

"My daughter-in-law who died had no family records. I always wished she'd had a genealogy. I'm grateful that Lesley is getting a wife this time who has."

Anna pondered Esther's reference to Lesley's late wife. What was this unknown girl-woman like? Had she been happy with the coldhearted, moody Lesley? Had she *chosen* to marry him, or had Esther arranged that union, too?

"You know nothing of the baby's maternal ancestors?"

"The whole family was killed in an Indian raid except Lesley's wife. But you are never to mention Lesley's first wife. Lesley wants to forget and make a new life for himself in the Oklahoma Territory. And you will help him do just that. The forgetting and the rebuilding." Her voice of deadly tidal waves and crosscurrents swirled about Anna's head, pounding at her ears. "You are a distant thing and cold. Worse than his first wife. But you can *learn* to love my son. It shouldn't be hard when you consider all that he has suffered and all that you will benefit by your marriage to him."

Anna refused the words a place on the shelf of her mental library. She hugged her Bible in a silence that dismissed the rest of the world. She could never feel totally abandoned now. Jason's absence at her leaving had an explanation, and he cared enough not to send her away penniless.

The Lewis children had never been allowed to handle the Bible or read it. Not because it was so sacred, Anna decided over the years but because of the inked-in registry it guarded like a courthouse. Jason thought only of the solace of the Scriptures when he stole it to her. *Or did he?* He had mentioned that it was his legacy.

Lesley's shrewd eyes and ruthless jaw lost their menace when Anna turned through the Bible with reverence, reading a treasure of verses here and there. One verse brought a half smile: *Lo, I am with you alway, even unto the end of the world.* She pulled a tiny splinter from the backboard of the wagon and marked the place. Separation from dear ones, the Horns, and the uncertain future could not crush her. She possessed God's own promise and Jason's brotherly kiss.

She tied the silver piece in the corner of a handkerchief and dropped it into her coarse bag. If they should pass through a town, she would buy stationary and a stamp to write to Jason as he had requested.

When her eyes began to blur with reading the Book, she laid it away for another day—a day when a mishap would take her to the guarded family registry and the surprises it held.

8

A Night in Town

*A*nna licked her dry lips with a tongue that trembled. Dreadful prospects ate away at her spirit like soul-termites, magnified by Esther's constant reminder that she would soon become Lesley's bride.

What would happen when the lumbering of the wheels, the clanking of the wagon chain, and the endless, weary hours of cramped riding came to an end? Philip Horn was impatient to reach his destination, but Anna's mind churned in a whirlpool of confusion when the thought came to badger her in the quiet of the night.

For days she had spent her energies dodging Lesley's advances and caring for the whimpering child, feeling sapped from both efforts. One wore her down physically, the other spiritually.

Days passed. And nights. Camp succeeded camp as the wagon lurched and rolled, leaving behind miles of dragging sand. It seemed that her family back in the land of sandstorms was separated from her by a thousand ages of time. All the happenings since the world began might have been wedged between her and the home she once knew. Even the memory of Jason bleached out to a faded blur. She felt like a very old woman now, carrying the weight of the world on her shoulders, rolling a great stone endlessly uphill.

On Saturday, they approached a town. Their wagon meshed with a congestion of others that made a living river of the hard-packed dirt road. Anna noticed that Lesley's mood brightened considerably. She hoped—a tremor ran through her body—she hoped he had no plans for her.

To Anna, who had never seen a town, the place seemed quite large. She didn't know there were so many people in the entire world! Jason had promised to take her to Lubbock, but her mother would not permit her to go with him. Such a venture would never have materialized, even when Jason got his hoped-for job.

The wagon slowed and the road filled with potholes. Anna gripped the edge of the sideboard as the wheels fell in and out of the washes, thumping along, throwing her about. She reached out her free hand to steady the baby.

Strange noises and smells pulled at her senses. Other wagons pressed so close to theirs that she feared they would be crushed. The boxed-in feeling made her feel sick and dizzy.

On the square in the slapdash town, vendors displayed their wares. Arrays of locally made food and merchandise lined the boardwalks: harnesses, milking stools, woven baskets, sacks of pipe tobacco, and bric-a-brac. Everywhere men were calling, laughing, jesting. The whole of it seemed crude to Anna. Jason would have protected her from this.

Adjacent to the open market were shops with meats being slapped on scales and clothes held up for size. Anna had not imagined that such extravagances existed.

Esther tried to look everywhere at once, excited and talkative. "Isn't this wonderful, Anna? We can actually go shopping and *buy* something! You can spend that dollar your mother sent you. There'll be so many things you'll see begging for it. But then, I'm sure you know all about shopping. This town probably isn't as big as the one where your family shops."

"I'm not a shopper, Mrs. Horn. But I do need some tablet paper and a pen. If you would be so kind as to get it for me, I'll keep the baby out of the noisy crowds. Babies need quiet."

A smoky-windowed tavern, trimmed with gaudy lattice work, caught the reflection of sunset, throwing back the sunlight while blotting out the evil brewing within. Anna gave an involuntary shiver. From the town's center, a network of narrow, sordid streets crawled away to unknown wickedness.

"We'll stop over here for the night," Philip announced. "We need a break from the desolate miles."

"Yes," agreed Esther. "Lesley needs the company of others his age. There's always dances and social affairs in these cities." She turned to Anna. "He'll go barter for you a bare-shouldered dress so you can go with him, of course. He'll want you to look like a modern girl, one he can be proud to show off."

Anna tilted her chin. "No, I'll just stay in the wagon, thank you."

"Certainly not!"

"I wouldn't like a dress that exposes my body. And I haven't the desire for dancing, Mrs. Horn. I wasn't reared that way. Besides, I'm too . . . weary. Please have me excused."

71

Anna heard Esther and her son arguing, their voices flinty in duel. Esther's voice rose angrily, then Lesley's. "There'll be another time, Lesley. The girl is tired. And she isn't accustomed to the outside world yet. Leave her be. You've plenty of time. No need rushing things."

She heard Lesley stalk off into society's colored world with a heavy stride, the heels of his boots coming down hard on the planks of a walkway. An unhappy frown settled over Esther's face.

Night fell and Lesley did not return. Anna awakened when he stumbled back to the wagon in the tiny morning hours. His breath told her he had passed the time in a taproom somewhere. She shuddered, glad she had not accompanied him. She determined that she would never go with him to such a place.

By morning, Anna remembered that she needed to buy writing materials to post a letter to Jason. She rummaged in her packsack for the handkerchief that held her money. It was gone. She removed the sack's contents one by one, but there was no trace of the dollar.

"I . . . I lost my dollar."

"If you dropped it, it likely went through a crack in the wagon floor," Esther said.

"I don't think I dropped it."

"I surely don't know what else could have happened to it, Anna. Money doesn't just sprout legs and walk off."

Anna bit her tongue.

About midmorning, they resumed their journey, with Lesley still sleeping off his hangover. Esther seated herself beside Anna, imposing her towering nearness. It was obvious that she wished to discuss something with her future daughter-in-law.

"My son doesn't . . . feel well this morning," she began. "If you had been with him, you could have brought him home before he became so . . . ill."

"Your son is a grown man, ma'am, and is responsible for his own actions."

"It's grief."

"Did he not act this way before . . . before . . ." She stopped, remembering Esther's command to never mention Lesley's deceased wife.

Esther reddened. "He's always been a bit, well, *rough*, but his first wife didn't try to help him overcome his . . . temptations."

"A real man stands tall without having to be propped up."

"Little you know about the world, lass."

"And less I want to know."

"You don't wish to marry my son, do you?" The ungarnished question wore no lace.

"No, I don't." Anna's answer countered with equal bluntness.

"But when you know my son better, of course you will." Esther made her decision aloud for Anna's benefit. Her tone and manner indicated that her decision was indisputable. "He wants to marry you now, but I've asked him to mind his manners until we reach the territory. With you being single, he can claim twice the amount of land. Lesley knows the law, but he's the impatient kind. He wants *what* he wants *when* he wants it. If *I* wasn't along to influence him, he'd marry you today, like it or not."

"I shouldn't like it."

"Your mother said she would be pleased to have you marry so well." Esther ignored the resolute set of Anna's mouth.

"My mother obviously doesn't care a shard what happens to me, Mrs. Horn. I came with you to work as a nursemaid for your grandchild, not to marry your son whom I do not love!"

"You're full of pepper, and that's just what Lesley needs to keep him in line. I wish his first wife had had more. And when they first married, she did. But gradually she began to live in her own little world. Lesley likes women with spirit."

Anna looked down at the baby she held. The child grew more beautiful each day. "I think, Mrs. Horn," she said, changing the subject, "that your son should give his lovely daughter a name. She is human, you know. And I think the law requires us to give her some identification."

Esther sighed. "I suppose so. I had hoped . . . I mean I had *feared* she wouldn't live to need a name, but it appears she is determined to survive in spite of everything."

"If I have anything to do with it, she will live."

"Then why don't *you* name her since she will be your daughter to rear."

Anna looked out toward the sandstone bluffs silhouetted against the backdrop of blue sky. "I think we should name her for her mother. Any woman who gives birth to a child should be given some consideration."

"I don't think Lesley would like being reminded of his first wife. They didn't . . . get on that well together."

"I doubt if it makes him one whit of difference, Mrs. Horn. None of his interest is invested in the child."

"Name her for yourself. You'll be her new mother. What about Annette? Or Annabelle?"

"No. We will name her for her mother. What was her mother's name?"

"I *hated* Lesley's wife's name. It was Modeane. I don't know what ever possessed her mother to tack such a name on a girl-child. We will not saddle the baby with such a ridiculous name!"

Modeane. Anna reached back and back into the recesses of her earliest memory to resurrect the sound of the familiar syllables. But the music of it escaped her, always just outside the grasp of memory's short fingers. Where had she heard that name?

"Then we'll call her Deana. That's a pretty name."

Esther shrugged. "I suppose that's as good as any. We'll need something to put on the headstone since she has lived this long. I'll still be surprised if she makes it to the territory."

"In the event she doesn't, Mrs. Horn, I will take the first stagecoach back home if you please."

Esther threw back her head in a snort of laughter. "And where, pray tell, do you think you might get the money for your fare? My dear, surely you know that you are destined to be my daughter-in-law. And I see that Lesley has his work cut out for him to manage you. Any other girl would realize that with land and a husband you will be the luckiest lady in the territory!"

The newly named infant cooed, while Lesley looked back with a bitter scowl, suffering a headache from last night's revelry.

In the days that followed, Anna ate and slept less and less. Like a heavy millstone tied about her heart, an icy sickening sensation weighted down her breast. Something awful loomed ahead. She felt it with a woman's intuition. Even her blood seemed to grow sluggish and cold. What could she do?

9

Prisoner

*W*hen the Horns made a brief stop at a small lake to replenish their dwindling water supply, it became apparent to Anna that she was a prisoner.

She climbed from the wagon and moved about to stretch her arms and legs while the baby slept. The air that blew across the lake filled her lungs, pumping new life into her blood. It had been a heartening day. Lesley had ignored her for several hours, and she found more verses in the Bible to give her courage.

As she walked the shallow shoreline, she made a mental evaluation of her reflection in the clear water. Her face was more chiseled than she remembered it, but it had lost none of its patrician qualities. Ringlets of golden hair played about her forehead and neck. Full lips and even teeth added to her girlish beauty. She had little to compare herself with, but none of the girls in the city were more fair featured. Outer beauty, though, had never been a priority with her; she was not vain. She longed to have an unblemished soul.

The lake's whispering waves lapped gently on the rocky shore. She wished this moment of peace could go on forever.

A young fisherman, hardly out of the boy stage, arose from his place on the short bank and started toward her with a friendly smile. He reminded her of an upright skeleton with scant pads of flesh added here and there to fill in the vacant places. She supposed Jason had passed through this bony half-child-half-adult phase at one time, but she could not imagine her own brother as gangling as this youth was.

Scarcely removed from the boundaries of childhood herself, she recalled the vacillating feeling of being a child in an adult body one day and an adult in a child's body the next. She returned the boy's shy greeting. He started to say something when his smile suddenly froze on his lips.

From out of nowhere, a pair of vicelike hands clamped on Anna's shoulders so hard that she winced with pain. The hands whirled her about. "Go back to the wagon right now." Lesley's eyes were cold yet ablaze with fiery flecks in their depths. "And you go back to your fishing, you no-good scoundrel," he snarled at the young man. "We don't want male company here. This is my girl." The frightened boy fled without a backward glance.

The shame that Anna felt at Lesley's rudeness to the polite stranger turned to anger. What right had he to forbid her the smile of a fellow human? She didn't belong to him! *Or did she?* Panic choked her. Somehow she must get away from this wagon, this vile man, and his conniving mother. When communication was cut off from the world at large, the situation could be nothing more than a prison for her body and soul. On death row, that's where her soul was. From that day on, she watched for her chance to make her break.

Esther sensed her change of mien and became her

guard, watching her movements with vigilance.

As they moved off the West Texas caprock and nearer the Oklahoma Territory, the terrain grew more wooded. The softer land knotted into unexpected little hills, and the solitary trees gave way to friendly clusters. By now, Anna's old fear had given way to a new desperation. She must escape. She *would* escape.

When they made camp one evening in a grove of gray-barked trees near a stream, Anna knew that the time had come for her to make her getaway. Her mind heaved with plans and details.

Tall butterfly weeds and thick gourd foliage would conceal her as she slipped farther and farther from the wagon to freedom. With her decision came a rush of spirit that fueled strength into her whole body.

Blackened firepits and charred logs revealed that this campsite was an old and oft-used spot. Anna could hide until Philip Horn's impatience—and the fear of being late for the land grab—drove him on toward the territory without her. And that wouldn't be long, she told herself. He would hardly stop for supplies of late, terrified of missing the opportunity of claiming free land.

After the Horn wagon was gone, she decided, she would find a way back home. Back to her mother and father, Willy, and Jason. Back to cactus and tumbleweeds and . . . sandstorms. Her mother would be ill-tempered about her return, but her father and brothers would welcome her, and they were a majority. If she could not get back to the plains, she would get . . . somewhere. Other wagons would be coming along. The future apart from the Horns, whatever it might hold, frightened her less than the present incarceration.

She rolled some hard bread and dried meat into an old petticoat and hid them under her shawl, watching for Lesley and Philip to go for wood and water.

With Esther pottering at the campfire and the men occupied, Anna kissed Deana goodbye and slid noiselessly into the trees.

A roar of rushing water told her that she was near a creek. It was a small one. She crossed it by stepping on stones.

Across the stream, she stopped for breath. She hadn't realized how weak and unaccustomed to exertion her body had become. Days of inactivity and a lack of nourishment —she had eaten little since she left her home on the Texas prairie—left her feeling light and dizzy after only a short walk. The climate was higher, the air thinner.

She slowed her pace but walked on, posting landmarks in her mind so that she would not become hopelessly lost and wander to her death. The tall trees, much bigger than any she had ever seen, made her feel immeasurably small. All these trees could look alike if one became disoriented.

When she supposed she had reached a distance where she was not likely to be discovered, she sat down to rest in some dense underbrush. Fatigue overcome her, and with her head pillowed on her arms, she fell into a drugged sort of sleep.

Daylight had dimmed when she awoke. *Something has awakened me! What?* Fear-induced hives popped out on her skin when the plaintive cry startled her from her half-wakefulness. *Deana!* She should be watching the baby! She shook herself to consciousness but could not remember where she was or why she was surrounded with thick brush. Where was the wagon?

The cry came again, this time more urgently. Anna looked about in bewilderment. Then she saw the petticoat roll beside her and remembered. She had come to escape the Horns' "prison camp." But who was crying? Someone needed help. It sounded like a baby's cry.

Anna moved toward the sound, searching along the ground all about her. Pushing through the bushes, she found a feeble spotted fawn, bleating for its mother. It was too weak to stand alone, and the soft pleading of its brown eyes struck a chord of pity in her heart. "Why, you poor little thing," she crooned tenderly. "Your mother has probably been killed by a hunter or a trapper." She cradled the animal's head in her arms and let the tears fall onto the silky coat of the orphaned deer.

Finally, the animal stopped quivering and rested its head on Anna's lap. While she poured her sympathy upon this motherless deer, a knife twisted in her conscience. The helpless fawn delivered an unspoken parable that left her shaken. A deserted baby that was much more important than a wild animal lay back at the wagon, desperately needing her. Without someone to care, Deana would suffer neglect and die! And with this knowledge, Anna felt that she would be indirectly responsible for a human life—or death—if she walked away.

Lesley didn't care whether the child survived or not. Nor did Esther. Both were too self-centered to think of anything but their own indulgences. Philip's shortcomings did not include willful neglect, but ignorance fell his lot. He would not even know that the child's life was ebbing away until she was gone.

The pitiful animal reached out a dry, pink tongue to

lick Anna's fingers. "You poor, unfortunate baby. You're thirsty!" She lifted him clumsily into her arms and staggered toward the stream she had crossed earlier in the day.

When Esther discovered that Anna was gone, she became frantic. "Go and find her, Lesley," she demanded. "She'll get herself hopelessly lost in this forest. I don't know how it is that I didn't see or hear her leave. She's been gone for more than two hours! There's bears and wolves and mountain lions in those woods. It seems to me she'd have more sense than to wander away. But sometimes I wonder if she has any sense *at all!*"

"She'll come back when the coyotes start to howl," sulked Lesley. "And if she meets her death, it's good enough for her! She's the most unpredictable girl I've ever seen. Now you see for yourself. Sometimes I wish you would have left her back on the plains where she belonged. If you would stay out of my life, I'd marry who I well please. And that would be a *saloon girl.* I hate goody-goody girls!"

"No saloon girl would cook and wash clothes and tend your baby."

"The way that baby is squalling, I think you'd best tend her before she drives us all crazy! I can't abide her crying. You said she wouldn't live, and she *did!*"

"That's why you need to go fetch Anna. I can't do anything with the child. You'll have sense enough to realize your good fortune when you get to the territory and settle down. And if you don't want Anna Lewis to cook your meals and bank your fires, there'll be plenty of other men who do. Remember that eager little fisherman. Now go! It'll soon be dark."

The look of green jealousy on Lesley's face pleased
Esther. Her ruse worked. She had to stir him up to bring
him to his senses. Without Anna, they'd all be in trouble.

Anna made slow progress back to the camp with the
spindle-legged deer in her arms. With each cautious step,
grasshoppers flew up like shooting stars. She ached all
over. Every few paces called for a time of rest. Two goals
possessed her mind: to save the deer and to get back to
Deana.

What she would do with the animal once she got it
to the wagon had not entered her mind. All that mattered
was that she defend two of God's favorite creatures—
children and animals. His delight in animals and His love
for children were evident in the verses she read.

The crash of heavy boots stopped her in her tracks.
She tightened her grip on the fawn when Lesley's face
appeared in a shadowy opening.

"What on earth . . . ?" His mouth spewed curses.

"I . . . I found this poor thing."

"All the worry you've caused us for the sake of that
scrawny animal?"

"He's weak. And lost."

"And there's not enough meat on that bag of bones
to make a decent pot of stew!"

Her scathing look only amused him. "I didn't bring
him for meat!" she retorted. "I brought him because he
had no mother and he . . . he . . ." She burst into broken
sobs.

"Stupid woman! It's almost dark, the kid is crying,
and Mama's mad." He turned back toward the wagon,
and Anna meekly followed.

"You found her, Lesley!" Esther almost shouted the

words. "Why, Anna, we thought maybe a wild animal got you."

"Looks more like she got a wild animal, Esther," Philip said dryly.

"He'll make us a meal, Philip," interrupted Esther. "We shouldn't scold her. This is the first thing she's tried to contribute to her keep since she brought herself along on our wagon. Can't you see how hard she has worked to fetch it for us? She even risked getting herself lost, snakebit, and mauled for our sakes. Why, she's as pale as the underside of a toadstool!"

"I didn't . . ." The ground moved toward Anna and then backed off.

"She's about to fall, Lesley!" urged Esther. "Can't you see that the deer is too heavy for her. Now take it, cut its throat, and bleed it good, and I'll cook it. It won't be much, but it'll make a mess of soup."

"No, please . . ." Would no one try to understand that she wanted the animal to *live*, not die?

Great sobs wracked Anna's body as Lesley snatched the frightened animal from her arms and shoved her toward the sound of Deana's incessant wails. "And for mercy's sake, go to that bawling baby in the wagon."

The fawn will die, she told herself. *But I'll see that the child doesn't. Even if it means being a prisoner to these dreadful people forever!*

10

The Dream

"*H*ere we are!" With the scrape of wheels on the leather brake, Philip Horn brought the team to a halt near the wide-bedded South Canadian River lined with cottonwood, willow, and dogwood. The stimulation of a dream realized gave the man a coltish delight.

"We'll winter here in the Chickasaw Nation." The map he unfolded, tattered and worn from being often creased and uncreased, threatened to fall apart. Anna wondered how he could read the dim markings.

"Bud has several crossings marked. There's Gillamore's Crossing about four miles from Purcell." He ran his finger down the listings. "Let's see. Barrows Crossing is just thirteen miles from Oklahoma Station. There's a railroad depot, a post office, and two large hotels there. Jenkins Crossing is farther up. And there's Silver City Crossing, Pikey's Crossing, Perry's Crossing, Downing's, Foster . . ." He studied the map some more. "I'm not certain which one of these would give us the best advantage. I guess it won't make much difference. From this direction, we'll have the jump on the people coming in from the north and west anyhow."

"Get us close to a town and *people!*" barked Lesley, defiling the pure air with his vile oaths. "I'm sick to death of the ghastly, deserted places you've dragged me over! I want some *life!*" Anna noticed that he had been ill-tempered since he emptied his secret jug several miles back down the trail.

"Yes, let's get as near a town as we can, Philip," sided Esther. "That'll make it convenient for purchasing supplies. Why make it difficult for ourselves?"

Anna cut her eyes toward Philip to see his reaction to their suggestion. The intoxication of journey's end dulled his perception. He yielded without contest to their manipulations, never suspecting ulterior motives in either his wife or son.

"We'll go on up the river then," he said.

A few other early wagons had come to wait. Philip found a spot that pleased Esther and Lesley where a clear, mild channel wandered back and forth between sun-bleached shores of riverbed. Anna surveyed the scattering of off-white canvases that made their camp in the vicinity. Did these settlers think their premature arrival would endow them with a sort of sacred seniority? To her way of thinking, they could all have waited until the miseries of winter had passed and as easily placed themselves in the lineup come spring. She did not understand the passion to "get ahead" of one's fellow man.

Lesley scarcely waited for the wagon to be established in a slight depression, sheltered from the wind, before he left the campsite for the life he sought in town. Anna felt relief when he was gone, glad to be liberated from his craven stares. He was gone three days before he returned, and when he did return, he snubbed them all.

Esther reasoned away his crudeness. "I'm glad we're out of that waste of lonely earth," she said to Anna as they arranged the wagon and the makeshift tent Philip raised for wintering. "Lesley didn't take to the desolate plains at all. It was the . . . awful silence. Especially after he laid Modeane there. And those long, darkening stretches . . ." she shuddered. "His temper will improve here. He likes *peopled* places."

"That's because he can't face his own soul, Mrs. Horn. He doesn't want to be alone with his real self."

Esther narrowed her eyes. "You are a hardhearted and unsympathetic young lady," she accused. "You will eat those very words when you are married to my loving son."

Lesley's absences grew longer and longer as winter approached. The days became shorter and colder. Great agitated clouds piled and rolled and mushroomed in preparation for bad weather, and frost silvered the morning grass.

Somewhere Anna lost track of time. It seemed a thousand lifetimes had passed over her head since she left her home on the high plains of Texas. She had come away a mere child; she would return—if she returned at all—an aged and spent woman.

Every day Philip came to camp with a babble of new excitement. "Game is plentiful here, Esther!" he crowed. "Today I found tracks of *nine* different animals! Panther and wildcat and bear and deer and coyotes and wolves and ducks and turkey and prairie chicken."

"Panthers? Bears? Wildcats?" shrieked Esther. "Now, Philip, if any of those predatory creatures come around here, I'll have you take me right back to California!"

87

"Unless you're lucky, you'll never see a one of them, Esther. They are just as reluctant to see you as you are to see them."

"Leave me unlucky."

"Some of those animals will provide us food all winter. I know just how the Israelites must have felt when God sent the manna and quail."

Another time he brought his glowing statistics and spread them out. "Guess how many varieties of trees grow in this area!"

"Why, I wouldn't have a notion." Esther's lack of enthusiasm did not daunt him. "We had quite a variety in California if you will think back."

"Not nearly as many as we have here! I found burr oak, walnut, hackberry, pecan, cottonwood, persimmon, elm, locust, dogwood, and willow. Why, Esther, Bud told me this was pure paradise, and he didn't miss it an inch!"

Then Philip went into Purcell, and Anna heard Esther asking about the town that took so much of her son's time and attention. They stood outside the tent talking. "Lesley spends more time there than here," she complained.

"It's a railroad town, Esther. Raw and elemental—a typical wild and woolly infant of a place. There's amusement of all sorts. Women and dance halls and shows. It has poker houses and they don't even try to hide their sins. I saw a couple of swindlers gambling right out in the street. And they say bootlegging does a booming business at the hotel there. There was some underhandedness going on at the livery stables, too, but I never figured out what was brewing. I'd never have known if someone hadn't dropped me the word. There's sharpers of all kinds, they say."

"Lesley's apt to make him some money, then. He's always been good at chancy games. He has a quick mind. What does the town look like? Would you compare it with San Francisco or Los Angeles?"

Philip laughed. "No, Esther. The town doesn't even have sidewalks or street lamps yet. The lights I saw were from the hotel and dance hall. There's but a few stores now. The building of a good town takes time—like the building of a man. It'll get more manners. It has a grand location. There's a high hill just north of the city with a view all up and down the South Canadian River. You could most nigh see clear to here."

"Is it . . . dangerous there?"

"Most everybody carries a gun, if that's what you mean. Revolvers or rifles or shotguns. Those guns sure look cross, but some who carry them look like a stranger to the weapon. Leaves you to think some tote them just to look tough. I dare say some of those gun-toters have never fired a shot in their lives."

"You didn't answer my question."

"Yes, killings are frequent. There's no law in Purcell except the deputy U.S. marshals."

"You don't think Lesley will get himself killed and leave the baby and . . ."

"They don't kill a man if he doesn't cross them. My guess is that Lesley doesn't cross them. I'd say he's *with* them most of the time. I'd worry more about him killing someone else when he's had too much to drink if I were you."

"I wish he would stay out of the town."

"He wants people, he's got them. The town is filling up already. Lots of folks are coming up the old Arbunkle

Cattle Trail that follows the course of the new railroad. That rail runs all the way from Arkansas City in Kansas to Gainesville, Texas. We're living in a modern world, Esther. Someday you will live in a grand, roomy ranch house. Lesley will have his own place, but there will be plenty of room for Lesley's baby and the nursemaid with us."

"Oh, Philip, I forgot to tell you! Anna and Lesley plan to be married when we get our land."

"Lesley and Anna . . . *married?*"

"I've known it for some time. She's bonded to his baby, and her mother said she can cook, too. Can you beat that?"

"When did they decide on that? He's hardly been civil to the girl!"

"I think they made their decision somewhere along the way. Back when he found her in the woods with the fawn, maybe. He knew then that he needed a mother for his baby and that she needed protection."

"Will her folks be agreeable? I promised her father that I would see after her like she was my own daughter."

"Oh, quite! They were afraid she would be a hopeless spinster on that prairie! How could she ever have met a gentleman stuck off out there? They will be beside themselves to see her marry into a good bloodline like ours."

"Then what's the delay, Esther?"

"*I* suggested that they wait until *after* the land run so that Anna could claim her some land, too."

"I had forgotten. Very wise counsel."

"But how can Lesley court Anna if he's gone into town all the time, Philip?"

"If you'll resurrect his first marriage in your mind, you'll know it doesn't take much wooing for our son. When he's ready, it'll be sudden like. And since you asked him to wait until we are on the land, he won't bother until then. Then he won't let his shirttail hit his back until he's wed."

"Don't you think the girl favors Lesley's first wife just a bit?"

"No, I can't see any resemblance at all except maybe her eyes and her ways. But the child is beginning to take on the nursemaid's looks. Strange. They say it happens that way sometimes. If you live around a person, you begin to look like them."

"Anna's a pretty girl."

"Well, if that's what she and Lesley want, I'll be agreeable. Maybe another marriage will settle Lesley down. I declare, he's run reckless with those thirsty outlaws ever since we got up here. I do wish he would tame himself down."

"Of course he will, Philip. He just needs time. You said yourself that a man needs time to develop—just like a town."

"Pity the wife if he doesn't."

Anna wanted to stop her ears. A haunting fear slowly fermented into torture and dried her mouth, leaving her with a strange tendency to swallow. Her skin felt cold and too tight for her bones. As long as Lesley's depraved lusts were abated in the wicked frontier town, she would be free from his passions. But someday . . . A pain like a stab of a cold knife shot through her heart. A surge of hysteria came, but she refused to let it stay. If she panicked now, she would be less equipped to face the unknown future.

91

She thought she might never sleep again, but night came and with it a drowsiness that fogged her troubled mind like warm breath on a cold mirror. In the comforting cocoon of sleep, she dreamed about home and her brother Jason. In the dream, he handed her the family Bible. "You will learn about God in this book—and about *yourself,*" he said. "Don't marry Lesley Horn, Anna. He isn't an honest man. He's a rat—a rat—a rat. Why haven't you written me? I gave you a dollar for paper and postage. Come home, Anna. Come home."

Home. A warmth spread into her veins, a tingle of gladness. The feeling recalled her girlish love for her brother, and she wanted the dream to last forever. She had so much to tell Jason! She needed to explain that she had lost the money. But the sound of Jason's voice lost its power and faded, leaving her empty and lonely.

When she reached the shores of consciousness, there were tears on her cheeks.

11

Call of the Heart

"Tell Maw I've ridden into town on some business, Willy." Jason clinched up the girt on Jesse, the youngest of the pair of saddle horses. He gave the buckskin a friendly slap on the flanks.

"Can I go, Jason?"

"No, you stay here."

"Is somethin' wrong? You ain't been actin' like yourself since those people came and took Anna away with them."

"No, Willy, I haven't been myself. There are just some things that bear on a man's mind and soul. Some things are hard to live with, boy."

"You didn't like Lesley Horn, did you?"

Jason was silent for a while, his eyes on the morning sun caught in a web of clouds. Then he spoke slowly, picking his words with care. It was important that Willy not think he carried a personal vendetta against Lesley Horn —or anyone. Willy must realize that there was a principle involved. He must be taught that people were not to be hated—but the evil within them was. Such a task took hand-picked words.

"Lesley Horn hadn't the stuff of a man in him, Willy. As I see it, there are only two kinds of men—real men and false ones. A real man is brave and a false man is a coward. There's no in-between. A real man lives clean and honest. A coward cheats and lies.

"I'm thinking there are some men who have no truth in them. A man without truth is not a free man. He's bound by his own self-deception. The truth is what makes a man free.

"Lesley Horn didn't shoot square with me right from the start. I haven't any respect for a man who talks out of both sides of his mouth."

"Our Anna wouldn't want to marry a coward, would she, Jason?"

Jason turned his head away, a dull, unplaced pain growing more intense. His unseeing gaze reached to the northern skyline where the wagon had disappeared nearly six months ago. "No, she wouldn't want to. But innocent girls can sometimes be tricked—or forced—into something they don't want to do. By dishonest men. Lesley hasn't any ambition except to satisfy himself. That always puts chicken feathers on a man."

"Did Maw know Lesley was a coward?"

"I'd rather think she didn't."

"What about Paw?"

"Paw never knew . . . a lot of things."

"When shall I tell Maw you'll be comin' back from town? You'll be in for supper, won't you?"

"I'll be in when I'm through with my business."

"Couldn't you wait one more day about goin', Jason? I don't like the looks of th' clouds. Paw said his bones were hurtin' like it might be stormy."

"I'll be okay." He looked away again. "But Willy . . ."

"Yes?"

"If I don't . . . get back . . . always remember what I said."

The impatient horse started as Jason put his foot in the stirrup and was running before he swung his leg over the saddle. Willy watched his brother boil away across the flats fitted to the saddle, moving with the stallion. He turned to his play in a distracted manner.

The dry prairie air still held on to winter's chill but hinted at spring. If one was moving, the wind cut deep. *Some things cut deeper than the wind,* Jason thought. He pulled his kerchief tighter about his neck and rode hard.

He felt regretful about leaving in this clandestine way, but he had waited as long as his heart would let him to check the post office again for a letter from Anna. On each supply run for the past half year, he had slipped away from his father to the mail window but had found no letter waiting. Now worry badgered his mind like a canker sore. No word from Anna was not good news. If all was well, she would write. He had given her money for supplies and a stamp. She had promised to post him a message when she reached the territory.

His mind somersaulted back over the months to the day of the sandstorm—back to memories he didn't like. His mother had not understood the clash of spirits. His father thought he was rude to the guest. And Anna was puzzled, failing to grasp the reason for his indignation. But he knew Lesley had been drinking before he ever disembarked and set his inflamed eyes upon Anna. He was an abusive man, cruel to animals and heartlessly withholding the healing love his own helpless infant needed.

95

They'd had quite a discussion, he and Lesley. Lesley knew how he felt about Anna marrying him. Lesley had promised that the choice would be hers, that he wouldn't impose himself upon Anna. But Lesley wasn't trustworthy. His word meant nothing. And Anna was innocent and naive.

He doubted that Lesley's possessiveness would favor Anna with the privilege of writing home if he should discover her attempts to do so. But surely Mrs. Horn would take Anna's part. Jason set his jaw hard. Why had fate brought the Horns by at such an inopportune time? Just when he planned to have a talk with his mother about Anna's future . . .

Usually, the city limits of Lubbock brought a breathtaking thrill to Jason. But there was an odd embarrassment, too, when he felt scrutinized by the city dwellers, who were much more experienced in matters of business than himself. The contrast between city and open range, even in a matter as simple as clothing, was almost alarming. However, he had a few friends among the less proud, more noble-hearted young men his age. His outdated and patched overalls seemed not to matter to them. Here he culled the thought of Lesley away. Lesley, with his modern clothing and careless attitude, would fit right in with the crowd that shunned him. Overgrown boys might be judged by their outward appearance, but real men weren't.

Jason remembered the childish excitement that came with his first trip into town. New to the high plains, he and his father made the trip to stock up on general supplies. Scarcely out of knickerbockers, he felt very grown-up in the rush and noise of the bustling city. He recalled the men with high top hats in the company of round-faced, soft mouthed ladies with their low-piled hair. The weathered, whitewashed stores. The lank brown loungers that leaned against the rails and about the doors of the building. He would never forget a giant of a man with the hawkish face in sheepskin chaps. He wore high boots with long, cruel spurs. But what impressed Jason was the Colt revolver far to the back in his belt.

He and his father were obliged to spend the night to negotiate all the details of their business and have a saddle repaired. He could still feel the nest of down-soft pillows as the two of them crawled wearily between sweet-smelling linen sheets at the hotel. Jason wiggled his toes under the satiny covers and revelled in the luxury. "Does this mean we're rich now?" he had asked his dad, and Richard Lewis had laughed deep.

Above the bed, the framed picture of the grand hotel itself looked down upon them. Thick rugs, fit for a king, stretched almost to the walls all around the high, spacious room. Jason lay awake for a long time wondering if heaven would be furnished more lavishly.

He got his first look at a comic strip (his father called it a funny paper) the next morning, drank his first soda, and saw his first pianoforte. He felt he'd lived a dozen lifetimes since then, but a tingle of apprehension had followed him through the years. Today, though, the thrill was gone. Would he ever again feel the delight of his boyhood?

He slowed at Main Street and looked to the right, then to the left. Joshua, the blacksmith's son, threw up a friendly hand blackened from the handling of the forge tools. Jason returned the greeting. He liked Joshua, who was younger than himself by two or three years. The young man was of solid muscle, solid character, and solid honesty. *Anna would like Joshua,* he thought. *I had planned for her to meet him.*

The inner magnet that pulled him to the post office limited his visit with the apprentice smith. "I'm expecting a letter from my sister," he told Joshua. He leaned forward in the saddle, and the horse put a forefoot forward with a quiver of anticipation. "She took passage with a family going east to help with a motherless child." He straightened his broad shoulders and tried on a smile but found it a poor fit.

Joshua tilted his head in response. His set of even, white teeth and dark, curly hair made him look even younger than the age of manhood he had just attained. "Lemme know," he grinned.

When Jason arrived at the building designated as the mailhouse—a small cubicle with a metal-grated window marked "General Delivery" and some numbered slots made of wood—he found a hand-lettered sign that read: *Out to Lunch.*

The sun suggested that it was well past lunchtime already, but there was nothing to do but wait. Jason came to town for the sole purpose of checking for a letter here. He leaned against the front of the building, alternately propping one foot and then the other behind him for support.

A ragged, barefoot newspaper boy limped down the street, one stubbed toe tied with a dirty rag. "Extra! Extra!" he chanted, dispirited. "President Benjamin Harrison sets the date for the Oklahoma Land Run. Read all about it!"

Jason fumbled in his pocket for a nickel. "Here, sonny! I want a paper," he called.

"Sure, mister!" The boy forgot his sore toe in his hurry to exchange a paper for the coin. "You innerested in somethin' like that?"

"Very."

"President signed the papers to open up that land on April 22. They can have it all. I'm stayin' right here in Lubbock and be a sody jerk!" He flitted off to hawk his papers with his nasal "extras."

With eager hands, Jason unrolled the paper and devoured every word of the information. People came and went, paying him little heed. The president, the periodical said, signed the documents on March 23. The land would be opened up for settlement in just a few days. Jason stored the data in his mind and folded the newspaper, but still the postman had not returned.

Two girls passed, painted-faced girls who slanted their gaze toward him in a seductive way, as vain as the ostrich feathers in their ridiculous little hats. Even their laughter revealed their inner emptiness. Jason looked on them with pity, grateful that Anna would never be like them, even if she were exposed to their environment. Anna had the makings of a lady; she had a lady's heart.

Across the street, the telegraph office clattered out its messages. A doctor's shingle hung on the building that was its neighbor.

"Waiting for the postman?" someone asked. Jason jumped at the sound of the voice.

"Sorry. I didn't mean to startle you." The wizened man and his volume didn't match. "Just wanted to say I saw the mister that gives out the mail down at the saloon earlier. Don't rightly know if he was delivering a parcel

99

or if he was having himself a drink."

"I suppose he'll be back soon."

"I wouldn't count on it, sonny. When all the mail's posted for the day, he considers himself dismissed. He may not come back until locking-up time."

The old man tottered on down the street and Jason continued his wait. Was the old gentleman trying to tell him there was no mail? If there wasn't he needed to be on his way home so as to arrive by sundown. The clouds might bring moisture, and his mother would be angry if he delayed supper.

He had never been in a saloon and had no desire to enter such a place now, but he needed to find the postmaster. If there was no letter, there would be no need to disturb the postal worker further. If there was, surely the man wouldn't mind discharging his duty by returning to the office long enough to hand out a letter to a customer pressed for time.

As distasteful as the idea was, Jason decided he must check in the bar to see if the postman was still there. He turned and headed down the street in that direction.

The tavern danced with sound: the chant of gamblers, the ring of coins flipped onto the counter, the ribald laughter of those who had inbibed from too many tankards. A dark frown creased Jason's face. His father would not like for him to enter such a wicked place—for any reason. But the inquiry would be short and he would be out of the smoke-filled den of iniquity in a matter of minutes.

The thin door opened with sudden submission to Jason's resolute pull. He squinted. Why would any proprietor want to keep a place so dark?

Still trying to adjust his vision to the dim interior,

he saw a tipsy patron nudge his partner. "Who's that?"

"Don't know. Ain't no local. We might hit him up for a loan. My money quit before my thirst did."

"By the looks of those rags he's wearing, he's worse off than we are."

"Yazz! Yessiree!" The man grinned stupidly.

Jason ignored their caustic comments and made his way past stained, clothless tables to the bartender. "I'm looking for the postmaster," he said. "Does he happen to be in here?"

"You looking for me, fellow?" A big, red-faced man in a blue conductor's coat with brass buttons moved toward Jason.

"I came to town to see if there's a general-delivery letter for Jason Lewis."

"Gents! Must be expectin' a letter from 'is bonnie!" sniggered a pot-bellied, carp-eyed man lifting a half-empty glass. "Wants it pretty bad to come *here* askin'."

"Let's see now. Lewis, is it? I'm—"

A gravelly voice that reverberated across the room cut his words short. "I knew I'd find you here!" A towering, bloated bully of a man pushed his way through the front door with a crash. "I came to settle the score!"

As Jason turned, the pistol cracked out its deadly shot and found the wrong target. The room filled with smoke and the smell of burning powder. A scream of protest arose against the senseless murder of an innocent man, and then bedlam broke loose.

A soft rain started—as if the sky shed tears for a guiltless man's death. And back in the adobe hut on the prairie, Corine Lewis paced the dirt-packed floor, straining worried eyes to look down the road at short intervals

101

as dusk settled over the plains. Once she imagined she saw Jason coming, but it proved to be only a dust devil—a whirling sand-funnel hop-scotching across the wilderness in the wake of the spring storm.

"Now what did he tell you, Willy?" she pressed again and again.

"You ain't listenin', Maw. I told you he said he was going to town on some business and that he'd be back when he was finished."

"Why didn't you ask him if he'd be back for supper?"

"I did, Maw. He said he didn't know, but if he didn't get back . . ."

"But if he didn't get back, what?"

"Aw, nuthin'."

"Willy, do you know what sort of business he went on?"

"Honest, I don't, Maw. He just seemed in a powerful hurry and powerful worried about somethin'."

"Well, I suppose he'll be in before long."

But Jason did not return.

12

Jana

*R*ain pummeled the sandy wasteland for a week. When the weather cleared, Richard patiently pointed out to his distraught wife, Jason would come home. He was holed up somewhere waiting out the showers. The ground would dry fast since moisture disappeared quickly in the porous soil. "We get too little rain to be complainers, Corine," he reminded.

But when the rainfall let up and his prediction proved unfruitful, he saddled the dappled gray and took himself to the city, leaving Willy to see after his mother.

The first place Richard stopped was at Watson's blacksmith shop, where farm equipment, wagon wheels, broken tools, and odds and ends of nameless things waited to be repaired at the forge. He knew Jason kept company with Joshua most of the times he went to town, and Joshua might be able to offer helpful information as to Jason's whereabouts. But Mr. Watson said that his son had been called away to work on an out-of-town job and would not return for two or three days. He ran grimy fingers through his tousle of black hair. And no, he had not seen Jason himself. And yes, Joshua did mention seeing Mr. Lewis's son and it seemed that he said he was on his way somewhere. But he had forgotten where. He was sorry that he could be of no further assistance. And if Jason dropped by, yes, he'd tell him that his father was in town looking for him. Give the family his regards.

Next Richard went to the livery stables. If Jason had prolonged business in the town—though he could not imagine what it could be—he may have lodged the horse at the stables. But the ruddy-faced groom shook his head. "Been no young man with a buckskin stopped while I was on duty. Haven't even seen one stepping around on the streets."

Jason had no money for a hotel, but it could do no harm to check. Richard asked at the front counter of the establishment where he and Jason had spent the night more than a decade ago. He remembered it as if it were yesterday. The same timeless pictures, now smothered in dust, hung on the lobby walls: Jesus holding a sheep; the newborn Christ child in a manger; the crucifixion; Jesus praying in the garden. Sand, tracked in by many feet, had taken its toll on the carpet, wearing its nap thin. The plush chairs, their colors fading, now showed signs of fatigue.

The day clerk ran a finger down the registry of guests who had signed in during the past week. "Lewis, you say?"

"Jason Lewis."

"We're out of luck, I'm afraid, sir. There's no Jason anybody or Lewis anybody on the books. What did he look like?"

Richard pondered the question. He had never been called upon to give a description of his son. Jason was just Jason, still a little boy in his father's mind, a little boy asking, "Paw, are we rich now?" But the added years had made his legs longer and his voice husky.

"He'd stand just short of six foot, I'd say." Richard rubbed his chin to think. "Or mayhap a little over. Young-uns grow up so fast. He has darklike hair that makes a deep wave in front on account of a cowlick and eyes as brown as a dried-out mesquite bean in the winter. He has a sort of crease in his chin that makes him more strikin' than most." As an after-thought he added, "And he's just turned twenty-three years old."

"What was he wearing, Mr. Lewis?"

"Wearing?"

"What sort of a suit did he have on?"

"He hadn't no suit on. He had on overalls held up by suspenders and a worsted shirt." Richard pulled his bushy brows together. "And brogans."

The proprietor gave a nervous cough. "No, Mr. Lewis, I don't believe your son has ever been here."

Richard knew he dare not go home without some word of Jason for Corine. But how was he to find the boy? Must he stop strangers on the streets and ask them one by one if they had seen his adult son? And would they not consider him a poor witless fool when he inquired for a man old enough to lead his own life, as if Jason were a runaway child? The curious look from the hotel manager was enough to discourage a random quest.

He rode the length of Main Street and back again, trying to decide what to do. Then he tied his horse to a hitching post near the town's square and walked aimlessly. Two tittering girls cut their wanton eyes toward him and pointed. "Remember the young man dressed like that old fellow?" whispered one. "I've always wondered what one of those creatures would look like all dolled up in frock coats and top hats. The young one was right good looking."

Embarrassed, Richard moved into the opening of a store only to find himself sandwiched between counters of women's forbidden garments. Flustered and disconcerted, he ran like a frightened chaparral bird when a saleslady started toward him.

Now completely disoriented, he leaned against the clapboard building to get his bearings. His mind whirled. Where to from here?

"Lost, mister?"

Richard jumped.

"Seems I'm getting good at scaring people," the dried-up miniature man expressed with loud regret. "I scared a young man that looked like a back model of yourself right about the same spot a week or so ago."

"You did? What was his name?"

"I didn't ask, sir." The little man's big voice echoed from the building's low overhang. "He was looking for the postman, he said. Seemed he was expecting a letter from some girlie."

Richard blushed. If it was indeed his son, he wouldn't wish the whole town to hear and think him in common correspondence with a girl. "Do you know if he got the letter?" He muted his tone, hoping that the old man would do the same.

"I couldn't say, sir." The words seemed to thunder louder than ever. "My Samaritan duty was telling the young patron where to find the postman."

"Did . . . did this young man have dark hair and brown eyes?"

106

"That pictures him just right."

"And was he wearing overalls?"

"You mean saggy britches held up by . . . by straps?"

Richard winced. The deafening sounds could surely reach to the city's boundary. "Yes, sir."

"I believe that might have been what he had on."

"That, mister, was my son. He seems to have lost himself in this place. I'm his father and I have come to find him and take him home with me."

"I'm not sure you will, sir."

"What do you mean by that?"

"I don't want to be the bearer of ill tidings."

"Ill tidings?" Richard turned white around the mouth, a black dread clutching at his mind.

"Well, sir, after he left this spot where we stand, he went to the bar. I saw him go in but never saw him come out."

"That young man couldn't have been my son, then," Richard said, raising his own volume to exonerate his son before the world. "My son would not enter such a defiled place."

"Don't you suppose that is exactly what the prodigal son's father thought, too?"

"But . . ."

"Do you want to hear the rest of the story—in case it was your son—or don't you?"

Richard gave a meek nod, desperate for any clue, good or bad. "Please go on, sir."

"There was a shoot-out that day in the saloon, and a young man was murdered in cold blood. Seems nobody knew who the man was or where he hailed from. It's all pretty hush-hush. But the outlaw that did the crime admitted himself that he got the wrong man."

"You're . . . you're saying it was my boy that was shot?" Richard slumped against the wall for support. His breath came in short gasps. "My . . . Jason?"

The shriveled man shrugged. "I don't know if it was your son or not. His body was never identified. He wasn't known to the bartender. The postal worker was hit, too, and ain't never regained his senses. The law closed down the joint and the owner skipped town. Ain't much left for the officials to go on to solve anything."

"They . . . they've already buried the man that was killed?"

"Had to. Undertaker wouldn't hold him out any longer. Put him in a pauper's grave. Out in the cemetery. County paid for the funeral." He talked in earsplitting phrases. But Richard no longer cared who might be listening.

"I can't believe my son would darken the doors of such a place."

"No. Your boy—if it was your boy I saw—didn't pass for a salooning kind. It wasn't for the low life that he went there. I told you he went there *on business* to see the postman." The withered man was shouting now.

"Is there anyone who could give me more information?"

"Nobody's talking it. Ain't good for business in our town. If people hear of senseless murders, they'll take their business somewhere else."

Richard stumbled away, dazed and sick. He called on the undertaker but learned little. The dead man's face had taken a bad hit, the coroner said, with powder burns and the bullet wound, making the victim nearly unidentifiable. He offered few details and hurried Richard away.

On his way home, Richard detoured by the graveyard. The newest grave, its fresh earth mellowed by the recent rain, swelled in a long and narrow mound. Its simple dignity, bare and unadorned, fit the brevity of the life it represented. No name graced the cheap wooden stick of a marker, and with a horseshoe nail from his pocket, Richard scratched the name "Jason Lewis" on the untitled stake.

A half-crazed sob escaped his lips. "Jason! My son! My son! How much more of my heart can be covered over with dirt and me still go on living?" An hour of agony passed before he thought of a greater anguish: how would he tell Corine of the tragedy?

Devoured with exhaustion and raw grief, he climbed back on his ground-tied horse and turned her toward home. Most of the trip back across the prairie he never remembered. Shock and misery met, letting moments of vacant darkness leap in and blot out all rational thought.

When the mare came to a halt, Richard focused his eyes on Corine's bulky frame in the doorway. Wide-eyed Willy tried to see around her. How could he break the news to them?

"You didn't find Jason, Richard?" Corine's voice seemed to reach him from far away.

"N-no."

"Richard! Richard! What has happened to our son?"

"He's . . . he's dead, Corine."

"Dead?" Corine moaned when a low back pain sent her to her chair. A look of terror crossed her russet face.

"Quick! Help me to bed, Richard! Willy, you run to the barn and stay until I send for you!"

Willy skittered away like a flushed pheasant.

Two hours later, a tiny girl lay in Corine's arms. "Bring Willy in to see his wee baby sister before she passes on, Richard," she said. "I hope with the last breath of this one, the good Lord sees that I have been punished enough for sending Anna away and occasioning Jason's death."

Richard sent Willy to his mother, but he stayed outside and let the darkness move in around him. His head throbbed with a new dread. The shovel propped against the stuccoed back wall seemed to mock him.

"I . . . can't dig one more grave." He slid his hand over the smooth-worn handle and kicked at the metal spade. "Please God . . . not for a girl . . ." Tomorrow, he told himself, there'd be another grave to dig on the sand-bleached desert. A sunless cradle for his beautiful little daughter.

But the child struggled and lived. Richard named her Jana. For Jason and Anna.

13

To Be a Man

A smeared gray underlined the horizon. Willy let himself out the door with animal-like caution, careful not to disturb his parents. Nothing must deter his plans.

He harnessed the horse and skirted the house, giving it a wide berth so the sleepers could not hear the thud of hooves. Stars still drenched the sky, stars that seemed to open and shut. He looked up at them. It was somewhere around five o'clock. Leaving at this hour would bring him back by early afternoon.

A hurriedly scribbled note waited for his mother on the washstand. He had gone for a ride, it said, and would be back for supper. She would fuss, predictably. And she would be angry when she learned of his trip to town alone. But there were some things a boy had to do that even a mother did not understand. It was not a matter of being dishonest, disloyal, or disobedient. It was simply following a higher call.

Willy had to find Jason's grave. There were things he wanted to tell his brother, things that he could discuss with no one else.

In the day's prelude, he found beauty and healing in the wide-flung and mysterious prairie, gravid with spring. The cacti, pearl-vague in the darkness, were transformed to imaginary sentinels that stood at attention as he passed by. They made him feel patriotic, as though he should salute.

Hatless, he liked to feel the fingers of the wind comb through his earlobe-length snarl of untamed hair. A lover of nature, he grew heady with the smell of the desert's spicy unknown scents and its thundery silence.

He rode hard, aware that after dim dawn day came on fast. With the first stippled rays that always introduced the rose-red sun to a new day, he should be well over halfway to Lubbock. He'd been as restless as a hound off scent since his father had returned with the news of Jason's death. He'd gone through all the mortal stages of the loss of a loved one: disbelief, anger, bitterness, and grief. He'd been on guilt trips and soul searches. Now he felt his stomach muscles untangling inch by inch. To see his brother's burial place—to be close to him—would somehow soften the shock of reality.

The new baby commanded much of Corine's attention. She was a winsome infant and Willy loved her. He was not jealous, but he felt a certain loss of the childhood attention that had been his before her birth. The event pushed him farther along the road to manhood, and he faced the transition in a way that he felt would have made Jason proud. Jason expected him to be a true man. Before Jason was killed, he talked to Willy as if he were already a man, not an unfinished one.

Jason always explained the *why* of things. Like the day he explained why he could not tolerate Lesley Horn.

Lesley, a no-account sort of person, liked to stay out all night and come in at noon for grub, leaving all the work to somebody else. He had the components of a coward. And Lesley didn't talk right or spit white. He wasn't honest with himself or anyone else. Jason had a strange way about him that when he pointed out the wrong in a man, it made the right seem better, nobler. He presented right as more *desirable.*

The sun broke over the skyline clear and beautiful, flooding the landscape with light. A cool wind blew, teasing the tumbleweeds and sifting the sand. The miles fell away under the mare's feet.

At the first cottage on the city's outskirts, Willy noticed a frail old lady bent like a folding fan over her flower bed at the end of the building that greeted the road. Her rough hands, too big for the rest of her, patted earth about a tiny plant. Tenderly she plucked one dead leaf, a flaw that no one save herself would ever have noticed, from her project. Her entire yard spoke of new life.

Willy stopped to ask directions to the cemetery. The woman raised her head and smiled, a genuine smile that seemed to turn her wrinkled face into that of a youthful girl. Her yellow-gray hair, tamed into place with a crocheted net, might have been golden girlish ringlets again. The transformation caught Willy by surprise. Only her face was old, he decided, not her spirit. Her eyes held ageless lights.

"Top o' the morning to you, sonny," she said. "How may I help?"

"Would you happen to know the way to the cemetery from here?"

"The cemetery? Know the way by memory, little man.

I've been there time and time again. And I can see by your eyes that you've suffered a recent loss yourself. Your mother, perhaps?"

"No, ma'am. It was my brother. He died . . . not long ago. I didn't get to go to his buryin', but I wanted to see his grave."

"Why certainly." She looked at her large, calloused hands. "All my family is planted there," she said. "I guess that's why I like to work among the growing, living things. It gives me a sense of balance, you might say."

Willy nodded.

"A cemetery is not much different from my flower garden, though, is it?"

"I wouldn't see any likeness, ma'am."

She chuckled. "When those bodies are put in the ground, my boy, they're not going to stay there. They'll bloom again somewhere on resurrection morning on the other side of Jordan!" Her work-worn hands cupped around a shoot as gently as if she cradled her firstborn. "I think I could do better with these flowers if I didn't have such bulky hands." She gave a music-box laugh.

"I think your hands are just the right size for you," Willy said. And he meant it.

"Go visit the grave, but don't forget my flowers," she said. "North to the water tank and then straight east to the edge of town."

Following her instructions, Willy rode directly to the graveyard. But once there, he forgot the flowers and the resurrection. The child in him found nothing to mitigate the ugliness of the burying ground, nothing to cushion its harshness. He found himself choking back sobs that threatened to wrack his young body.

114

The freshest grave . . . that would be the one. Torn with emotion bigger than himself, he tumbled from the mare's back and threw himself prone on the barren mound. He cried until his strength was spent, his eyes swollen and red. The dusty hand he swabbed over his eyes streaked dirt across his forehead. He heard himself talking.

"I just wish you could tell me why this time, Jason," he wept. "You were so good, the best brother a boy could have. Why do the good have to be killed and the crumbs like Lesley Horn get to go on living?

"There was so much I was just beginning to learn from you about manhood. Now I'll have to learn most of it on my own except for Paw and God's help.

"I still remember what you told me about being a real man: that a real man is honest and brave and that truth is what makes us free. You left me with a lot to live up to, but I'm going to be a man you'd be proud to call your brother." He patted the grave. "I promise." He sat in thought for a long while, trying to imagine Jason beside him listening.

Willy stood up, still young in body but feeling somehow old. Giving up his hero had multiplied his years. He mounted the horse and slapped her with the reins. "Now I want to see where my brother was shot," he told the animal. The filly pounded her heavy hooves and whinnied. "Gid-ep!"

Joshua motioned for Willy to stop as he went by the blacksmith shop. "I've been wanting to see some of your family," he called.

Willy pulled the horse to a halt. "Whoa!" She snorted and champed her bit.

"Are you all alone?" Joshua asked.

"Yes. I came in by myself today. On business."

"Your Paw came by a week or so ago asking about Jason."

"I know." Willy dropped his eyes.

"Jason told me to give his family word that he had gone to the territory of Oklahoma to check on Anna. He was mighty concerned about her since he didn't get a letter in the mail. But he wanted his paw to know where he was so he wouldn't worry."

Willy shook his head. "There's no use telling Paw now. Haven't you heard, Joshua?"

"Heard what?"

"Jason is dead. He was . . . killed."

"Why no, Willy, I didn't know. I hadn't heard a word about it. I'm so . . . sorry." He choked on his Adam's apple. "When did your family get word?"

"About a week ago it was. Maw and Paw are taking it awful hard, too. And me—it about cut my liver out."

Joshua lifted his arm and wiped tears onto his sooty shirt sleeve. "Did you get word to Anna of his death?"

"We don't know how to reach her. I wish she had never gone."

"Me, too."

"But even if she knew, it would just be more pain for her. She was awful crazy about Jason."

"Well, Willy, if there's anything I can ever do to help, just come around. I know I could never fill the shoes of a brother like Jason Lewis, but we can talk when you're lonesome."

"That helps." Willy seemed at a loss to know what to do or say next. Then he smiled, a brave effort of courage. "I have a new sister, Joshua. She's awful tiny, but we believe she's going to live. Paw heated up jars of warm water and wrapped them in flour sacks and put them around her to keep her warm. And Maw's a changed woman. If Anna ever comes back, Maw will treat her better. Not that Maw was unkind to Anna, but she just wasn't *motherish* like a girl needs. This little girl that's been born has made a lot of changes in Maw's heart. It's helped Paw, too, to have another girl to take Anna's place. Paw missed Anna a lot. I hate it that Jason never got to see the baby or know about her. He'd sure love her—and she'd be nuts over him, too. Paw named her Jana for Jason and Anna."

Joshua accepted Willy's confidences with a pleased look. "So you are a big brother now!"

Willy sobered, awed by the new sense of responsibility. "Yes, and I've got to try to be as brave and as honest a big brother to *her* as Jason was to me. Jason told me how to be a real man. As I see it, real men are mighty scarce nowadays, and since Jason got knocked out of the game, I'll have to step up and take his place. And I'll do it. Or die trying."

With a wave to Joshua, the man in a boy's body rode away.

14

The Missing Book

"*F*etch me th' family Bible out of th' trunk and let me record our daughter's name and date of birth," Corine said, holding Jana to her breast. "Granny always told me if a youngun lived a fortnight, they'd live on to a ripe age. We finally got us a girl to write in."

Richard dug in the wooden chest, pushing aside valueless relics and musty, outgrown clothes. "Why do you keep stuff we'll never use, Corine?" he sputtered.

The dust that filtered through made him sneeze. "I can't find no Bible. The trunk has been rummaged through. Everything's topsy-turvy." His hands groped about the box's bottom.

"Well, it's in there. I've kept it in the same place since we first moved here. I've never seen a man in th' world that could find th' nose on his own face."

"It *ain't* in here, Corine."

"Here. You hold th' baby and I'll find it. Big as it is, it ought to be easy enough to feel. It couldn't be no place else."

Richard took the child and Corine lowered her heavy body to her knees for the search. Articles of sentiment sidetracked her hunt.

"Why here's the breastpin you gave me when we married, Richard! The one that belonged to your own mammy. Pity I don't live in town so's I'd have some place to wear it."

"I thought mayhap you'd pass it on to our Anna when she gets to marryin' age."

"No. I'll keep it for my Jana."

"A long wait you'll have."

"And look! The first slingshot Jason whittled out. Remember?"

"Um hum."

"I don't guess it's important that I keep this old hand fan. It's fallin' apart." Before she had finished, every item in the trunk was piled in a heap on the floor and commented upon. She gazed, with a perplexed frown, into the bare floor of the chest.

"I told you it wasn't there."

Corine's eyes blazed angrily. "And you're right. It ain't. There's only one other place it could be, Richard Lewis!"

"I haven't touched it, woman."

"But somebody has."

"Who are you tryin' to blame?"

"Anna. She must have stole it and took it with her. You said yourself that th' trunk had been rummaged through. She knew where I kept the Bible. She fished it out in a hurry and left with it."

"Now, Corine, you don't know . . ."

"See there. You have always made excuses for Anna. Just who else would have known where th' Bible was kept? Who else would have took it? Who else would have *wanted* it?"

120

"Anna did have a great yearnin' for God and good livin'. But I'm sure that she didn't mean it to be stealin'. She probably figured since you never read it that you wouldn't mind if she took it with her and read it."

"Takin' without askin' is stealin' anyway you read it."

"Why would you mind so much that she borrow it?"

"You ain't thinkin', Richard! It ain't the *Bible* part I mind. It's th' family names in the middle that I don't want her to find. When she sees, she'll know. . . ."

"I told you years ago that you ought to tell Anna the straight about her birth, Corine. I was afraid she'd find out."

"I was tryin' to protect Jason. And Willy."

"It wouldn't have made Jason and Willy no matter. They'd both love her no matter what."

Her hard, level stare was meant to wilt him. "Sometimes I think you ain't very smart."

"What's done is done. I don't doubt that Anna will bring th' Bible back with her when she's through workin' for th' Horns. Anna's not a thief. And she'll likely have questions that beg answers when she gets here."

"She . . . ain't plannin' on comin' back here."

"Why, of course she'll come back when she's through jobbin'. What do you mean?"

"She'll make her home with the Horns. Permanent."

"You didn't *forbid* her to come back, Corine?"

"No."

"Mr. Horn told me plain the very day he left that he'd see that Anna got back to us safe and sound when they were settled on the land and Mrs. Horn was able to take up th' care of th' child again. I took the man for an honest gentlemen." His speech was quiet and bitter.

121

"Anna plans to get married."

"To get married?"

"Yes. She plans to wed Lesley Horn."

"Lesley Horn?" Richard's lips twisted. "Our Anna marry Lesley Horn?"

"She couldn't do no better for a husband. Esther said so herself. Lesley is high educated an' knows his way about in th' world. He'll be rich when he gets his land and he's from good family stock. Esther said Lesley had such a way with women that he'd have Anna's head turned and her heart won over ere they left sight of this house. Esther said they'd have to stop and find a parson for sure."

"Oh, Esther said this. Esther said that. I'm sick of what Esther said."

"Be sensible, Richard. When could Anna ever have hoped to find her a mate stuck out here on this forsaken plain?"

"Corine, the Horn's son has the poison of sin and drink runnin' in his veins! Anna deserves better! Why, I'd rather see her live out her days on earth with no man at all than be cursed with the likes of Lesley Horn!"

"Calm down. You're workin' yourself up into a dither. I told you th' young man wasn't *himself* when they came by. That's all you got to judge by. He'd just lost his precious wife, and grief had rendered him most nigh senseless. Esther said he was a darling boy when he wasn't tormented with sorrow."

"There you go again. Esther said. I don't care what Esther said. But you got one word right: *boy*. That's the word that fits him. *Boy*. And he'll never be anything but a spoiled *boy*."

"I hope them very words come back to mock you."

"God be thanked that Jason didn't live to know about this. I'm a mind to go to th' territory myself an' warn Anna."

"She'll be married a'ready by now. It'd be a waste of time. You'd find her rich an' happy as a pig in th' sunshine in her new life with Lesley Horn."

"I wish I had known before she left." Bunches of jaw muscles worked in and out. "I'd never have let her go with that *rat.*"

"You would have kept her around until . . ."

"I'll always blame myself for her misfortune of goin' anyhow. It's a shame for a girl to have to work for her keep. I should have withstood th' whole bunch of you. Jason would have backed me."

"Oh, sure, Jason would have."

"Nothin' has gone right since Anna left!"

"Richard Lewis! How dare you say such foolish things. Th' good Lord up in heaven hears you. I brought you a baby girl and she's well—and pretty."

Richard ranted on. "And now Willy's all upset with life. I don't like him slippin' out and ridin' off on these dry plains and stayin' gone for hours. Seems I ain't done nothin' since I been on these forsaken plains but lose th' battle of tryin' to snatch children from death and our land from mortgage. I've seen a lifetime for every year I've spent here! And it was your idea to come. I can't see as Indian raids was any worse than this!"

"Don't fret yourself about Willy. Boys need roamin' time. He's out huntin' them ugly horned toads. I hate th' squatty, rock-gray things. They quiver and hiss at me. I can't understand why Willy loves 'em so."

"If he don't come in soon, I'm goin' to have a look-for after him."

"He won't like that. It's as if you're pryin'. Th' note said he would be in by supper, and he will. He's always kept his word like Jason. It's trust you got to have in a child. He ain't no baby."

"You have a lot of room to talk about trust."

Richard paced and worried, spent his spirit. In his mind, Willy was but a child, and many wiser and older had been lured to tragedy by the land's deceptive depth and distance.

But while Corine prepared the evening meal, the door rasped open, jarring the whole room. Richard jerked his head up and looked full into his young son's face, a face streaked where tears had made a path. The boyish eyes held shadow, but behind the shadows was a soft, subdued light. There was something different about Willy. Richard searched but failed to find this first bud of manhood.

"Where have you been, boy?" Corine shooed a fly out the back door with her tattered apron.

Willy looked away. "Off on a little trip."

"Tell us, son." Richard took up the query.

"I just went away to . . . think."

"It's a body's privilege to think to hisself, Richard. Leave th' boy be," Corine said. "Did you find any toads today, Willy?"

"I wasn't lookin' for toads."

"Now, Willy," scolded his father, "I don't want you wanderin' off like this no more. You must understand that we've done lost too many of our family, and your goin' off for hours at a time puts a worry on our minds."

"I won't need to go again for a long, long time. It's

just somethin' I had to do, Paw."

Richard started to say more, but Corine interrupted. "Willy, do you know wherever th' big family Bible went? Th' one that we keep all the records in?"

"It's in th' trunk."

"It ain't. I guess Anna took it. Th' chest was all mussed."

"No, Maw, Anna didn't take it."

"She'd'a been bound to. It's gone. I've emptied clean to th' roots where it always nested."

"I know for sure Anna didn't take it with her, Maw. I watched Lesley Horn load all her pack. It was th' pack you handed him, and Anna didn't take out nothing else besides."

"Bibles don't just flutter away."

"Don't fault Anna. Lesley said some bad words and vowed he wouldn't put in one more thing that belonged to her—not so much as pin. And he meant it. You saw her yourself when she loaded on. She didn't have no Bible in her hand."

"That's right, Corine," echoed Richard. "Th' Bible was too big to hide. Now I'll appreciate it if you wouldn't be accusin' Anna of things she didn't do."

"Then what could have happened to that Bible? It frights me to think someone could have snuck in while I was hangin' clothes on th' line. And our Jana layin' on the cot helpless. Why, they could as well have got her."

"I don't know what happened to the Bible, but I don't think we've had intruders, Corine," Richard said. "If a body was aimin' to rob something, it sure wouldn't be God's Holy Word! They'd likelier want my old gun." His eyes went to the shelf above the window. "And it's still there."

125

"Was you plannin' to read th' Bible, Maw?" Willy asked.

"No. I was needin' it to put down Jana's date of birthin'."

"And Jason's death?" Willy's reminder came out in a husky, man's tone that indicated his changing voice.

With jolting revelation, Richard knew where his son had been. The little boy had vanished. In his shoes stood a young man.

15

The Old-Timer

*E*sther had tolerated the winter on the ambrosia of Philip's wild promises. He exaggerated these promises to utopian proportions, feeding his wife with thoughts of plowed fields, broad furrows, and yellow grain shimmering in the Oklahoma sunshine until he established a mirage of handsome farms and ranches just across the South Canadian River. At the least signs of depression, he inflated her hopes anew.

The months had worn away the sharp pains of agony that Anna felt with the first separation from her family. Even the lingering ache of memory had faded to a thin gray.

With the cold, miserable weather of 1888 marked from the calendar, wagons seemed to come in droves. Anna had no idea there were so many people in the world. Humanity gathered here in all tongues, all garbs, all colors. And all odors, she thought. It seemed to her there must be thousands of them, lined up mile upon mile. "Where do they all come from?" she asked Esther.

"From *everywhere*. It reminds me of the California gold rush," Esther told her. "Lesley will love it and so

127

will I! I can hardly wait for the *cities* to be birthed with their great universities, parks, schools, churches, and libraries. I hope we live right in the capital city. Why, it wouldn't surprise me if Lesley should become *governor*. Can you picture yourself the governor's wife?"

"I'm afraid not." Somewhere along the line, Anna decided, fantasy had conquered Esther's logic.

"You'd have to have some schooling, of course. You need a bit of refining."

"I think if your son aspires to be governor, he should choose someone else for a wife."

"Oh, no, my dear. His mind is settled. The baby would never adjust to anyone else now. She's so attached to you, she can hardly bear for you to be out of her sight. And it won't be long now. The wagons are coming in at such a frightening pace! Did you see that six-passenger phaeton that came rattling in today?"

"I don't believe I did."

"Must be rich folks. They have a big new wash pot swung beneath and buckets strapped on the sides and end. Look. There it is." Esther pointed to a large wagon with crudely-painted lettering on its gleaming canvas that read "Bound for a Home."

"I believe they brought a whole general store with them. I've been watching them unload. Besides those two cows and the hog-backed cow pony, they brought tubs, a grub box, a sewing machine, straight-backed chairs, a rocker, a cookstove, a plow, a rake, a scythe, a hoe, and a big stone jar full of seeds of all kinds to plant. I guess you'd call that faith in the future." She paused to catch her breath. "I can't imagine such prosperous folks living in a sod hut just to get land, though."

"It's hard to imagine."

"And yesterday I saw a honey-colored surrey with a fringe. Why, they even had a brass-button chauffeur with a white shirt and all. Up from Dallas, somebody said. Now that's my kind of people! I wanted to visit with them, but I haven't seen them today. I dare say they'll quarter up at the town hotel until a few hours before the signal to run for the land."

For some of the pilgrims, Anna had nothing but sympathy. An aging man with watery gray eyes and skin the color of old ivory passed and tipped his battered bowler hat to her while she heated weak broth for Deana over an open fire. He reminded her of a winter tree, doggedly holding to a few reluctant leaves to hide its bareness. She wondered that he would spend borrowed days in this uncharted wilderness. Why hadn't he stayed near the burying ground of his ancestors in a softer land?

Perhaps he sensed her sympathy and concern. Or maybe he was lonely. He often stopped by while she worked about her camp to give a friendly greeting. She came to look forward to his daily visits. "One of the hordes of rudderless people without real purpose here," Philip Horn labeled him. But Anna knew better. The old fellow had a history, a past. And a future.

The camp children learned that the elderly man had a twangy jews'-harp from which he extracted doleful discords. Oblivious to the disharmony, they flocked after him, pied-piper fashion, begging for music and stories. Relieved mothers shooed them to him from underfoot. He became a camp teacher-hero for the youngsters.

As he stopped to speak to Anna one morning, a flock of clamoring fans gathered about him. "I'm going to tell you a tale based on my missionary work," he promised the children. Then to Anna he said, "I think you'd like to hear my story too, little lady." His words shot out like marbles around brown snags of teeth.

"Oh, I would love it!"

"Then I'll tell it here so you won't have to bring your baby away from your own camp. Isn't this a wonderful garden, lady? Look across yonder to that buffalo and blue-stem grass. Why, that's the finest grazing and planting place on the face of the earth. Just feast your eyes! I've traveled over the United States and have never seen anything more glorious! Hundreds of acres as level as a floor and waist deep in pasture grasses. Oh, if I was just a young man again! All the land I need now is six feet to sleep forever in. But this land sets my clock wishing to tick backwards!"

Anna laughed and the children grew impatient.

"Oh, yes, yes, yes . . . my story. Now let's pretend this story happened far away across the ocean in Africa when I was a young man. Maybe twenty. Maybe twenty-one. That was a land of uncivilized men then, fierce and bad. But I wasn't scared of the bad men, because good never has to be scared of bad, children.

"One day I was moseying along through the jungles, minding my own business and wondering what I could find to do good for someone when a band of cannibals came out of the bushes after me. There must have been at least ten of them, all carrying spears. Those spears looked ten feet long!

"I saw that I was outnumbered ten to one, and I had no way to defend myself. But I could run like the wind.

"Well, children, I began to run, darting in and out

130

of the brush. I ran about a mile, zigzagging. Then I looked back. Here came the wild men. So I ran another mile. Here they came, not gaining ground but not losing either. We ran for an hour or so just like that. A cat-and-mouse sort of chase, you see.

"I was needing to catch my breath and getting mighty thirsty, so I closed my eyes and I prayed a little simple prayer asking my heavenly Father to help me. When I opened my eyes, lo and behold, I was face to face with the biggest herd of elephants I had ever seen in my life! What could I do then? The elephants were in front, the cannibals behind. I was surrounded.

"Well, children, the cannibals got close enough to start throwing those wicked spears. The spears scared the elephants, and they stampeded in a wild frenzy. They came running right toward me, and I thought sure I would be trampled under their massive feet. I jumped up in the air and caught one of them by the ear and hefted myself up onto one of those wrinkled gray backs. It began to move. So I hopped to another back. Then I hopped from back to back across the whole herd, putting that mass of angry animals betwixt me and my adversaries. Now what do you think about that, kiddies?"

The shaggy-headed children clapped. Anna wondered what part of the account was fact and what part was fiction.

"Now run along home, laddies and lassies, until tomorrow. When you hear me play my harp that'll mean I'm ready to tell you another story and you can come a-running." The little ones scattered to their shelters.

"You were really a missionary?" Anna asked.

"For a fact. A missionary and a preacher. I've traveled far and wide. Where there's people, I go. The new settlements will need a parson and there's still a little wood on the wheels yet. I'm going to stake claim on some land and build a church."

"I see."

"We're all of one yardage, girlie—the black, white, red, brown, and yellow. Death is our common denominator, and we all have a bit of eternity in us. But our attitude helps make a great difference in our destinies. The attitude is the helm of the soul. Our attitude is part of our *spirit*. The wise man said our spirit is the candle of the Lord. That's what He uses to look into our hearts—our spirit. Yep, little lady, our attitude will help determine where we spend our hereafter."

"I . . . hope my attitude is right."

"Straight as a string, girlie. Anyone who loves children and takes time for old folks can't be too far off course. And you don't seem to find it a chore."

"Oh, not at all, sir. It's the proud people I have problems with."

"You and the Lord."

"Children are innocent."

"I love children myself," he said. "Never had any of my own. Lost my wife after just a year of wedlock. Never remarried. How old is your child?"

"She doesn't belong to me, sir. And I don't know for sure just how old she is. Under a year."

"You're not married?"

"Not . . . yet."

"You have plans then?"

"The family I am with has made plans for me to marry the son."

"Not the young man that comes in from Purcell now and then?"

"Yes, sir. That one."

"But he's not fit for a nice young lady like you. He hasn't a right attitude and he flirts with the town women. I wasn't born yesterday. My eyes may be dim, but they haven't failed yet. Just last evening, I passed a saloon and heard the tramp of boots to the rhythm of cheap music and saw that very young man come out on the arm of a disgraceful girl, all tipsy and a shame to behold. No, you don't need that one, girlie. Take it from me. There's better for you."

"I'm afraid I don't have much choice, sir."

"No choice?"

"The marriage has been arranged for me by my mother—and his."

"And this is his baby you care for?"

"Yes, sir. I've taken care of her since she was newborn. The only peace and happiness I have is when I hold her in my arms. I confess, sir, that I love her so much I think I'd marry him just for . . . for her sake."

16
The Letter

*T*hunder banged from cloud to cloud, starting with the closest and charging away to the farthest, frightening Deana. Boiling black formations swallowed more and more of the sky. Twisted threads of lightning burned through them. A cloudburst like a wall of solid water tumbled down. It seemed that it would never let up.

"The river is rising fast, Esther!" Philip shouted. "We'll have to move!"

Frothing red water surged into a broad expanse of churning menace in its mad eastward rush, sweeping trees and uprooted soil along with it.

"But Philip! If the river stays up like this, we can't get across to get our free land!" whined Esther.

"We've a few days yet, Esther. They've just recently broke the filibuster in Washington. I heard them talking about it up in town. Grover Cleveland is no longer president and folks say that the new president who took his place, Benjamin Harrison, will issue us a proclamation right away. It'll be to his favor. Most folks allow that he will give at least a thirty-day notice, though. The river will surely be settled down by then."

"I hope, Philip, that we haven't waited all this time in vain! If I have endured this horrid camping and then we don't get good land . . ."

"If we can't cross, then neither can anyone else."

"But you forget that people will move in from the east and the west and the north while we sit here waiting for the river to tame."

"I promise, Esther, I'll get our land if you just won't panic. I'll cross the railroad bridge or swim or something."

"No, no, Philip! You might be killed."

"Bud will see that we have our share of the best land in Oklahoma. If you *must know,* he and Lesley already have our spot picked. Now let's get this camp moved. We haven't time to squander."

Even the worthless Lesley came to help break camp and move it up the bank from the imminent danger. He was sullen and edgy. His eyes pierced through a bold, dark mask to betray his vile nature. The reddish gleam in those eyes seldom left Anna's body, but he gave his child no attention at all. Anna was glad when the move was complete and he took himself back to his vices.

There was little to do but huddle inside the tent and wait out the storm—and try to allay the baby's fear of sudden noises. Dragging hours of confinement gave Anna leisure not afforded in fairer weather, and she reached for the Bible Jason had brought her, ashamed of her longstanding neglect. She felt an urgent need for its comfort now as the chilly, damp atmosphere weakened her morale.

The Book slipped from her hands and fell open in the middle, face up. She recovered it, puzzling over the squatty little knots of letters written in its midsection.

The penmanship was her mother's, a fair hand for her poor education. Names of ancestors on both sides of the family sat on the parchmentlike, yellowish registry. Long since deceased forefathers listed here were strangers to Anna. Her mother had given her little insight into the family's past. Indeed, it seemed a hush-hush subject in the home. And now that she was miles removed from her family, what mattered? With disinterest, scarcely above boredom, she let her eyes travel down the columns of people she did not know.

Her father and mother's wedding date was recorded and, a year later, the birth of Jason. *Jason.* She would never see her beloved brother again. Trapped in her loveless marriage, she would live out her days here until death released her to a better land. He would marry, too, and she would be but a story to his children. With food and raiment, she'd try to be content with her lot in life. And she'd have Deana. It wouldn't be what Jason wished for her, but he'd never know if fate treated her poorly.

The names of four more boys made stairsteps toward the bottom of the page, their dates of birth and death one and the same. Some of the names she had forgotten, the more recent ones she remembered. Wedged among them was Willy's name—William Edward Lewis—the last survivor.

She searched the page until it became a blur. Her mind tried to absorb the discrepancy. Her own name was not listed! Why? She should be on the roster after Jason.

A thousand thronging sensations came and went. Then the confusion subsided and she knew. She did not belong to the Lewis family at all! Why hadn't she awakened to this truth long ago? Corine Lewis wasn't her mother. The mirror should have clued her in. The revelation brought many answers and raised even more questions.

She also realized why Jason had given her the Bible. He had wanted her to know that she had not been born to the Lewis family.

Who was she? Had they any claims on her? Or she on them? Horror edged into her chest with each painful recollection of the past. Corine had wished to be rid of her for years. When she left the land of sandstorms, hadn't something warned her that there was no turning back from the dread future? Yet locked away in some secret vault of her heart, she held an unreleased hope in reserve—a hope that as a last resort she could flee back to her family there. That last resource was now shattered, vandalized by a page that chose to ignore her name.

She had no family. Relieved of her presence in the home, Corine would never allow her return. The woman wanted only her own biological family. Anna was and always had been an unwanted intruder. She bit her lips to hold back a bitter cry.

Jason, the brother she idolized, was probably not her brother at all. He was just someone who showed himself a gentleman, kind to everyone, hoping that she might find happiness.

Of course she would never be happy now. If the chance ever existed, it was obliterated, erased from her existence this day. Jason thought he was helping by letting her know she didn't belong to them. He thought he was setting her free. But instead, the knowledge cut and hurt and bruised. Like a lopped-off branch, she could but wither and die inside. This wasn't Jason's intention, she was sure, but the damage was done.

This morning before she saw the register in the Bible —the sweet, cool, wetness of the dawn—was the last good she would see in her lifetime. The stars would from henceforth be cold and mocking. They would remind her of a meteor lost in orbit, destined to wander in the blackness of night forever. The thought crushed her. It was practical and cold. Even her dependable tears refused to come and bring relief.

Some infamy, some dishonor too terrible to repeat, must be attached to her beginning. Else why had Corine tried so hard to hide the truth from her all these years? Did Jason know? Surely he must. That is why Corine had made sure he had no opportunity to be alone with her: he might reveal the dark, ugly secret. Anna snatched at the mismatched pieces of the puzzle and put together a distorted picture of her own, a picture with sinister shadows and no sunshine.

With eyes closed, she picked back through the tangle of many yesterdays to reconstruct every word Jason said at that last parting. His kiss she now wished to forget; it was given out of pity. She relived the scene through to the finish and then jerked her eyes open. He had asked her to write to him when she reached her destination in the territory and address the letter to General Delivery. That was so Corine wouldn't know about the correspondence. It was the only request he made, and after she lost her money, she forgot about it.

He would want to know that she was aware that she was not his sister. The knowledge would absolve him of any further obligation to her. He'd been kind and had risked a tongue-lashing to get the Bible into her posses-

139

sion. The least she could do would be to send him a word of final thanks and forever close the gate between them. He was of noble birth; she of ignoble. Small wonder that Corine hated her.

Anna gathered the courage to ask Esther for writing supplies, the only favor she had asked from the Horn family since she had joined them. "Jason asked me to let him know when we arrived in the territory," she told Esther. Her face burned. "I should have done so before winter, but I . . . forgot."

"Yes, I remember now that you were going to buy a tablet in the first town where we took lodging."

"But I lost my money."

"One shouldn't be so careless. You never did find it?"

"No, ma'am. I had it tied into the corner of my lawn handkerchief, and even the handkerchief was . . . lost."

"Of course we must contact your family and let them know that we arrived safely. I supposed that you had done that long ago. I hope they are not worried."

Anna said nothing, but the burning of her face spread to her neck and ears.

"You write the letter, Anna, and I will have Lesley take it into town and make sure that it is posted right away. With these rail trains, the mail moves much faster than it used to."

Anna took up the pen, but her hands shook so that she could hardly write. The crisp message she put on the page bore no resemblance to her inner feelings.

She thanked Jason for the Bible with its family history. The disclosure, she said, made her know that she was not a part of the Lewis family and that their responsibility—whatever it may have entailed—ended with her

140

eighteenth birthday. They had been generous to bear the burden of her upbringing. She thanked Jason abstractly for his brotherly concern for her while she was in the home and then bid him a stiff farewell. She gave no hint as to her whereabouts, only stating that they had arrived at their intended destination without incident.

Lesley agreed to take the letter to the Oklahoma Station post office. Out of sight of the camp, he tore it open and read it. He held it suspended over the river's edge ready to drop it in but then snatched it back. The letter was formal, curt, tiecutting. Sending it would cause Jason discomfort. Jason thought too much of Anna, anyway. Lesley would like to picture him suffering. He'd send the letter for spite.

He patched up the envelope and bared his teeth in a demonic grin.

17

The Story

"Corine!"

Richard's face was haggard and drawn. Each trip to town for supplies became more dreaded than the one before. He no longer asked questions about Jason's murder. He wanted to hear no more. The town gossip left him confused and broken.

"What is it, Richard?" A white ridge showed around Corine's mouth. "What dreadful thing has happened now?" The shadows she invented in her imagination stretched longer than the substance.

"This." He held out a patched envelope plagued with dirty fingerprints.

Corine snatched at it. "Who is it from? Let me see."

"It belongs to . . . Jason."

"And you haven't opened it?"

"No. It's his."

"How ridiculous, Richard! You know Jason is dead. When . . . where did you find this letter?"

"The new postmaster flagged me down on th' street in Lubbock and asked me if my name was Lewis or if there resided any Lewises out my direction. When I said that was my name, he gave me the letter."

"Well, let's open it up and see what it's all about."

"I . . . . I can't, Corine, I ain't never opened up anything that didn't belong to me."

"Well, give it here. I certainly can."

Corine tore at the envelope. "Looks like it's already been tore into once."

"That's what I thought."

Corine unfolded the sheet without dignity and took her time reading it while Richard waited.

"Who is it from, Corine?"

"Anna."

"Anna? Why would she write to Jason in place of writing to you and me?"

"She had a secret likin' for Jason."

"Corine! Her fondness went no farther than that of a younger sister. All sisters make heroes of their older brothers. Just see how Jana already listens for Willy's voice! Does th' letter show a special affection?"

"No."

"What *does* it say, Corine?"

"It answers to a question. But it sure pulls up another wonderment just as big to take its place in line."

"Stop talking in riddles, woman." Richard always added "woman" when he was irritated or impatient.

"Anna is thanking Jason for the *Bible*. She said she saw the names in the center and she knows now that she ain't a part of our family. How and why and when he gave her our family Bible makes for galling questions in my mind."

"Jason gave Anna our Bible when she left?"

"It appears so."

144

"Why, Corine, Jason was nowhere around when the wagon pulled off for th' territory."

"It is a puzzlement, Richard. But it's evident she has the Bible, and if I read the letter right, it was Jason that fetched it to her."

"But why?"

"I knew if she ever got ahold of it, she'd be sure to find her birth not catalogued there. She added two and two. Now she knows we ain't her maw and paw. Nor Jason and Willy her brothers."

"You should have told her from the first yourself. It would have been less grievous for everybody."

"No, th' way I did it was th' better way, Richard. She might have got ideas that I was partial to th' boys over her if she had known sooner. And she might've got romantic designs on Jason knowin' he was no blood kin."

"Nonsense!"

"Why else would she send th' letter to Jason instead of one of us? But what-might-have-beens don't matter nohow now. Jason's gone beyond her reach."

"I think, Corine, that you should write and tell Anna about Jason's death. We're all th' family she's had since she was just a wee tyke. To me, she's th' same as my own flesh-and-blood daughter."

"You're not sayin' she means as much to you as our Jana?"

"Exactly. And I'll write her if you won't."

"You can't. She don't give no return address on th' back."

Willy crashed through the door panting. "Paw, a big cloud is a-west. Do you think it's a bad sandstorm a-comin'?"

"No, Willy, I don't think so. Th' cloud ain't th' right color. Just a bank for a shower, I'm thinkin'. And it may not even get this far."

His face relaxed. "I was hopin' it wasn't a sandstorm. Ever since those people came in the storm last year, I've *hated* sandstorms."

The outburst, so unlike the optimistic Willy, surprised his mother. "Why so, Willy?"

"Well, if there hadn't been a storm, they might not have lodged here at our house and took Anna away. Jason didn't want them to take Anna. He didn't want Anna to marry Lesley Horn."

"He didn't?" Richard furrowed his brushy brows until they almost met in the middle of his forehead. "How do you know he didn't?"

"He told me so! He said Lesley Horn wasn't a real, true man. He said *men* were honest to themselves and to others—and Lesley wasn't clean with either one. Lesley had his jug of spirits in the wagon hid from his own paw. He was a weakling, a coward! Jason didn't mind if Anna married, just so she married a worthy man. But Lesley Horn wasn't deservin' of a girl like our Anna. If you want to know what I think, I think if Anna hadn't left, we would still have Jason alive!"

"Why, Willy, Jason's death had nothin' to do with Anna. She was gone for weeks and weeks before he was . . . killed. You said yourself he went to town on business."

"That's so, but his business in town had something to do about Anna. I know it did! Joshua said . . ."

"What did Joshua say?" Richard moved his whole body to the edge of the split-bottom chair to hear.

"He said Jason was terrible worried about Anna when

he didn't get the letter . . ."

"The letter, Richard," Corine nodded. "He was expecting it. That's why he took hisself to town."

"I knew Jason was bothered, but I didn't know he was so . . . so dead set against Anna going." Richard shook his head wearily.

"Well, he was, Paw. The day they left here, he saddled up Jesse and followed after them. I know he caught them too, because I asked him. He said he talked to Anna, but he wouldn't tell me what he said to her."

"See, Richard."

"Corine, there was never a more innocent child than Anna. From the day Jason found her, she's been nothing but pure and sweet."

"Jason *found* Anna?" Willy captured the slip made in the conversation and bombarded his parents with questions. "Where did he find her?"

"It's a long story, Willy."

"You mean Anna isn't my sister?"

"No, Willy, she isn't."

"You might as well tell it all, Richard. It makes no matter now, anyhow."

"Before you were born, William, we lived in the New Mexico Territory down near th' border. You've heard us talk about that. We lived on some borrowed land that belonged to a family named Elliott. They owned a big rancho there and had a nice log home, well furnished. There were four children in the family. Three older ones and Anna was the baby.

"Anna was born three days after we buried th' first baby we lost to th' earth. Your maw took it badly, and it went hard with her to see Mrs. Elliott with a healthy

147

baby when her own didn't live. I guess that's only natural. It put a strain betwixt th' two women.

"We'd heard about Indian raids and we knew we lived in a dangerous area with th' possibility of a massacre anytime. Cochise was chief of th' Chiricahua Apaches, a dangerous tribe. Th' name was a horror to all of us pioneers. Ours was an isolated place. Some allow that Cochise had a right to be chafed since he had showed hisself friendly to th' whites once and they betrayed him. After that, revenge ate at his entrails night and day.

"All th' women that lived within a hundred miles of where we were got curdled blood when they heard th' Apache name mentioned. Your maw and Mrs. Elliott were no exception.

"Sure enough, the Indians struck one day about noon. Jason saw them movin' toward th' Elliott place in full war dress. Feathers and paint and all. Th' Elliotts were out workin' in their field, unaware. Being just a seven-year-old boy, he tried to think of a way to warn our neighbors to save them. He did a mighty smart thing. He ran into our cabin and got an old muslin sheet. He'd heard somewhere that Indians are skittish and superstitious. So he draped th' sheet over his body like a ghost and made moanin' ghost sounds to frighten them away from th' Elliotts.

"But raidin' Indians are lightnin' quick. They had already killed Mr. and Mrs. Elliott and th' two older children before they saw Jason and thought he was a haint. We never did know th' fate of th' third child who was outdoors, too. They must've captured her alive.

"Well, Jason ran into th' house and found baby Anna just wakin' from a long nap. She was two years old.

148

He brought her to your maw and me.

"After th' raid, your maw was afraid to live in th' New Mexico land any longer. She pestered and plied me day and night to move her away from there. We started back east and broke down right here, and we've been here ever since. We brought Anna along with us.

"Here's where you were born. Your maw thought it best to let you think Anna was your real sister. And anyway, to me she always seemed just like . . . ours. I put no difference in her and you boys."

"Did Anna know?"

"Not while she was here. We just got a letter sent to Jason that lets us know she found out."

"How did she find out? Did the Horns know?"

"No. Jason took her th' family Bible with th' birth records. Anyway that's what th' letter there indicates. She found out her name wasn't along with the others."

"So that's why Jason followed them. And that's why he wouldn't talk about it." Willy calculated aloud.

"Jason always wanted to tell Anna about her family, but I wouldn't let him," Corine cut in.

"Well, Anna was my sister whether she was born so or not. And I'm sure Jason felt the same way." Willy talked in his new man's voice.

"I think Jason felt that he should . . . protect Anna." Richard spread out his big hands. "And that's the story."

18

Clearing the Trunk

*R*ed caliche dirt clung scablike to Anna's skin. She missed the incohesive sand, the one thing she thought she'd never wish for. It seemed a dread paradox: the sands of her life on the Texas plains could be shaken off, but her unknown future here could not be brushed away. It would fuse and grasp in its doughy hold.

Each day now, Philip Horn pulled a small book from his pocket and studied the complicated symbols. "It's just days away now," he reminded. "We're fortunate that the surveyors left us a way to identify our claims. We will be locating in this vicinity." His finger came to a standstill on a marking that made no sense to Esther or Anna. "Everybody is waiting for the signal to join the hodgepodge of racers into the territory. Isn't this exciting?"

Some of the light had died out of Esther's eyes. She sighed. "It's a motley crew as I see it. Farmers, ranchers, adventurers, businessmen, cowboys and bad men alike all mingled up together."

"You have a mixture in all society, Esther," chided Philip. "This is said to be the biggest land rush of all time. It's the same with all frontiers. Even California. You've just forgotten."

That evening as she lay in the makeshift shelter surrounded by hundreds of land-hungry sojourners, Anna pondered what Philip said. Her mind retraced the journey from the cacti-infested wasteland to here, pointing out hills like giant frozen waves, lakes of sour-colored water, and rocky valleys. The map looped and turned in her mind and brought her back to her starting point, back to crooks and gamblers and loose women.

Many had trekked across the hills in open wagons, buggies, carts, and buckboards. Some rode horseback. Some walked. Farmers brought household goods, implements, stores of seed, livestock. They all swam across her mind and merged into a vague assemblage as sleep dulled her perception.

What happened next brought her from the drowsy fog with a start. She sensed more than saw the pitchy blackness of a shadow outside the opening of her tent. Her mind froze into solid-block panic, threatening to still even her breath. Should she scream for Philip Horn and incite a human stampede of chaos among the campers, or keep quiet?

She hadn't time for a rational decision before Lesley Horn moved into her room and clamped a steely hand over her mouth. Where had he come from? She had seen little of him for days.

"If you are thinking of a silly woman's yell, don't," he warned in a throaty whisper. "It's just me. I came to tell you that I have been out in the territory and have our quarter sections spotted. We'll beat the game. When the cannon roars, I'll jump out of the brush and stake my claim along with yours before the legitimate racers get a chance." He gave a gelid laugh. "Then we'll be married and we'll have twice the land."

"But in case I don't want to be your wife?" Biting sarcasm yoked up with Anna's fright, creating hoarse words that wobbled out.

"You must have a man in these wilds, Anna. For protection." His superior tone made her detest him the more. "Besides you need cheering up. You're much too serious for your own good. I might just cheer you up a bit right now." He moved closer. "Betrothed is as good as married." She could feel his hot, telltale breath against her cheek. He'd been drinking again.

Was there nothing, no one, to save her from this brute? *Lo, I am with you always . . . O God,* she flung the silent prayer toward heaven, *send Your angels to help me now!*

A calmness stilled her racing pulse. "The baby . . . is asleep," she said. "Please don't wake her. She will alert the whole camp with her wail if she is frightened."

"Who cares about the baby?" His growl disclosed his unquenchable passion.

And God, help me not to hurt little Deana, Anna implored, as she reached over and gave the infant a bump that awoke her suddenly and made her begin a frantic, high-pitched cry.

"Go!" Anna gave Lesley an imperative shove. "We'll talk about it later. When you return. The baby will awaken everyone around us if I don't get her back to sleep immediately."

Lesley drew back as if a marshal had appeared at the door with a warrant for his arrest.

"I wish there *was* no baby!" he snarled. "I never wanted her in the first place. She was my wife's idea. And

I wish I had no *mother*. I'd have taken you before now. Back at the first town." Suddenly he backed toward the opening as the baby's screams pierced the night air. "But I'll be back. And it won't be long. In a few days, you'll be my wife, *ceremony or not!*"

When I left the plains, Anna thought, *I hated the wind, the dust, the sun, the endlessness of the land. It seemed grim and ghastly, a heart graveyard. But now I would welcome a sandstorm that comes and passes so swiftly. Here the storms linger on and on.*

On the morrow, Anna said nothing to Esther about the rendezvous. The terrors of the night seemed less ominous by day's bright light.

"I hope Lesley doesn't get himself arrested," Esther fretted to Philip. "I hear the army has sent out fourteen companies to keep the claim jumpers out. That's what they're calling the people who go in ahead of time and get their land located."

When Philip scoffed at her fears, she turned to Anna. "Oh, Anna, I wish we had never come to this horrible place!" she said. Anna felt real pity for her.

But for Lesley, Anna wasted no sentiment. She found herself thinking she would feel only relief if he should be arrested and imprisoned. A desperate wish became both father and mother to the thought. If he should be apprehended, there'd be no marriage. At least not for a while. Good fortune, though, had seldom befriended her, and she had little hope for such a turn of luck now.

Esther grew more irritable each day. "I don't like it here," she told Philip. "I want to go back to California. I felt better when I could breathe the ocean's salty air. I want palm trees instead of these gnarled oaks."

"We'll be settled on our beautiful land very soon," he cajoled. "And the first thing I will do is build your lovely house. If you want palm trees, we'll plant palm trees. *Anything* will grow in Oklahoma." Anna noticed that his promises grew more radical with the passing of time.

But Esther pulled her mattress into the wagon and seldom came out. A blanket of black depression stretched over her. Philip wearied of trying to placate her. Anna attributed her ill humor to her worry over Lesley.

When the heat of feverish blood burned her body for more than a week, Philip left the campsite and returned with a comfortable-looking woman, her neatly plaited hair coiled into a snakelike S at the back of her head. The woman looked at Esther, her face a study of grave concern. She poked a tentative finger into Esther's swollen side and Esther cried out.

"She won't live the night through," the woman said matter-of-factly. "She's bloated up. Probably something busted inside her and poison has set in already. I can smell the gangrene. Get yourself ready for a burying." If Esther heard the news, she paid no heed.

Esther's last breath came just before daylight. Anna sat clutching Deana and watched death rob the body of its soul. Deana would never remember her grandmother, but Anna would never forget her.

The neighbors helped to dig a hasty grave in the caliche paste of soil that seemed to Anna capable of gluing a soul to the earth on resurrection morning. Anna requested permission of Philip to ask the old-timer to say some words of farewell over the lifeless body.

With Esther's remains properly disposed of, Philip set off to find his son, giving Anna instructions to go through Esther's belongings. Her clothes should be given to the kind lady who had ministered to her in her dying moments, Philip said, as a sort of payment for her services. Everything else could be burned. It would lighten the wagon for the run.

The unexpected death of his wife, he told Anna, would necessitate her immediate marriage to Lesley so that she could fully manage the Horn family. She would take Esther's responsibilities. He would live with her and Lesley so that he could police Lesley's abuse of her and the child when he drank too much. He admitted he'd done this in Lesley's first marriage. Then when Lesley had sufficiently matured, he would join his brother in whatever craft the relative occupied himself. He would not seek another wife for himself, he told her.

When he had gone, Anna sorted through what he had said. If she only had herself to account for, she reasoned, she would run away—even at the cost of death. She had never feared death, only life with Lesley Horn. But another life depended upon her. Little Deana, who had struggled so valiantly to survive in a cold, motherless world, deserved a chance to grow up with love. No one else would sustain her, and Anna could not risk the child's health for her own selfish escape. If marry she must, she would wrap her emotions in a tight circle around the child whose subsistence was already entwined about her heart in an inseparable way. Given a free choice, she decided, she would choose to stay with this brave, precious child. Lesley Horn or no Lesley Horn.

While the baby napped, she pulled Esther's worn trunk from the front of the wagon and released its rusty lock. Old clothes that smelled of a peculiar mixture of

mothballs and lavender lay on top. These would go to the
nurse lady. One dress, a smaller, ecru-colored pongee,
must have been Esther's wedding dress. Or Deana's
mother's? Anna dropped it to one side; it wouldn't fit the
larger lady and it might suffice for her own vows—for
vows she *would* have. She would not live with Lesley Horn
without a lawful ceremony.

The dress was of a high-collared, modest variety. It
was something she might have chosen to be married in.
Something Jason would have liked. Mentally, she slipped
the dress on and smiled. Then a vision of Lesley standing
beside her made her shudder. She lashed out at the mental picture with a frightened cry. Lesley did not *belong*
beside her.

In the bottom right-hand corner of the chest, Anna
found a packet of papers marked "Modeane Horn." Philip
told her to dispose of everything in the trunk, leaving it
empty for storage in their new home, but some sixth sense
urged her to look through the papers before she fed them
to the campfire. After all, what belonged to Deana's
mother belonged to the child. And there might be a keep-
sake she would want when she grew up.

So Anna leaned against the wagon's sturdy railing
for back support and untied the string from the stack of
folded papers. She sighed as she started to read, not
relishing the task. It was like looking into some ghostly
past, pulling the restful dead back for a personal meeting.
But she must do it for Deana.

19

The Revelation

$\mathcal{T}$he more Anna read, the more she wanted to read. A real person stepped from behind the smoky glass of Esther's word gallery of portraits that sketched her daughter-in-law. This young woman, released from prejudice, stood before Anna on her own merits. Anna liked this girl-woman with whom she could identify and whom she could admire. These writings were messages such as she might have written herself. She understood them and felt at one with the writer.

Deana's young mother, Anna decided, must have known that she would not live. Many of the pages were a sort of diary directed to her unborn child. Some were written neatly, as soldiers standing erect ready to fight any unseen battle. Other words staggered across the paper like the writing of a wounded warrior, apparently thrown on the parchment in great haste lest the writer be caught at her craft.

To my unborn child was the heading of one composition. It read: "I want you to know something of your maternal history. I am recording these incidents in the event that I should not be able to tell you the stories around the hearth or table when you are old enough to comprehend.

"We were a household of six surnamed Elliott—a grand old family with a strong taproot, an honorable tree. Father owned a prosperous ranch in the New Mexico Territory near the border; we had a nice log cabin and good land. Your Grandmother Elliott loved her children, her God—and your grandfather. Father was a man of integrity, prayer, and indomitable spirit. He taught all his children to be pure-hearted.

"We were working in the garden: Mother, Father, Julius, Logan, and I. Mother sent me to check on the baby, who was asleep. Before I could get inside, the Apache Indians attacked. It was a terror such as I shall never forget. They came silently, with no forewarning. One instant they were nowhere in sight, the next they were there to kill and plunder, their bodies scarred and painted.

"Mother knew the danger of Indian attacks. History held too many tales, and our isolation made us the more vulnerable. So she pinned our property deed to my petticoat every morning. Somehow she thought that being a girl child, I would be the least likely to be harmed by the savages in case of a raid.

"When Mother saw the Indians, she screamed for me to run. In obedience, I turned from the house and fled. The Indians killed all my family, but I made it to the main road, and a band of wagons going west took me in. I'm sure the Indians burned the cabin with the baby inside after they took what they wanted. That was their pattern. My little sister's name was Anna Michelle. Mother let me help her choose the name."

Anna dropped the page. Her hands shook as a dream-

160

like memory, too vague to take shape, came and faded again as dreams will. Could Lesley's late wife have been her own sister? Could Deana be her sister's child? This was storybook stuff, not meant for real life. If indeed she was a member of Modeane's lost family, was it happenstance that she sat here reading from her sister's handwriting, or was it by divine arrangement?

She lifted the next page from the lot, eager to learn all she could. "I was taken to California with the wagon train, never quite belonging to anyone anywhere. When I grew older, I planned to return to my land and a childhood sweetheart, a boy named Jason who lived on a section of our land. But who knows, perhaps the Lewis family was slaughtered, too. I have heard nothing of them from that day until this.

"A marriage to your father, Lesley Horn, was arranged for me by my foster family. I had never met the man. And since he is your father, I must keep his name clean before you so that you can believe the best. I hope that he can prove worthy of your trust, be you a son or a daughter.

"If I should die and these papers fall to you, guard the land deed. Unless Anna survived by some miracle, you will be the only heir to the property. The land is valuable for its 'black gold,' a substance the government will pay a great price for. . . ."

A light, washed feeling—almost a giddiness—passed over Anna's being as if the whole earth had been bathed in a sweet essence. At last, she knew who she was, and that newly discovered disclosure would hold her in any storm. She was of noble birth! She had a lovely heritage and could hold her head high!

Using the delicious bits and pieces as fabric, Anna wove a resplendent story—a story that she would pass on to Deana. Her own birth parents had been neighbor to the Lewises. Her sister and Jason were playmates who had exchanged kisses in childish innocence. Someday, they promised each other, they would grow up and belong together.

After the tragedy, someone found the youngest in the cabin sleeping. Almost the story seemed tangible and remembered. Was it Richard Lewis who found her? Or Jason? What size hands lifted her? Almost . . . almost she could see them.

Jason would have been old enough to recall the details. He *knew* she was not his sister. And his knowledge cost Corine days of worry when Anna began to blossom into womanhood. When the Horns came along, Corine saw the chance she sought to send her away from Jason.

Jason had never hinted that Anna was not a family member by birth. But Corine's jealous actions should have told her. Corine, brown and pudding faced, resented the fair-skinned, blue-eyed intruder into her family unit. Probably she had never wanted her in the first place.

Betraying no deeper emotions, Jason had treated her like a sister. Until that one kiss. Now she regretted the letter she had written and wished for postage to send another. If only Jason could know of her discovery! She had sent him no idea of her whereabouts. But by the time she could get a message to him or he to her, she would be married to Lesley anyhow.

Modeane's notes presented a freedom that set her mind in a dozen different directions. If she could only find a means of eluding Lesley Horn and getting back to her land, she could make a life of her own there. She would have some legal claim on her sister's child. She bound the deed into her clothing and closed the trunk.

Newborn joy lured her out of the wagon for a walk in the sumac-laden, honeysuckle-odored woods. She cuddled her niece to her body and found herself skipping along in the delightful intoxication of her fresh insight. Her heart took wings.

With a view of camp hardly lost, a hard-eyed man stepped from the thicket of trees and blocked her way. She stopped, frightened.

"Your name, madam?" he asked.

"Anna Lewis, sir."

"And the child's name?"

"Deana Horn."

"Your child?"

"No, sir. My niece."

"Does the child belong to Mr. Lesley Horn?"

"Y-yes."

"Then I'll have to ask you to return to your camp."

"Why, sir? Is there a problem?"

"Mr. Horn hired me to see that you didn't leave . . . with his child. He seemed to think you might try to escape. Was that your intention?"

"Surely you can see that I have no baggage. It would be sheer folly for a lone girl, a scant eighteen, to try to follow an uncharted course with a baby!"

"Why are you here?"

"I only planned a short walk for myself and the baby. For the spring air, sir."

"Sorry, madam. My orders. It wouldn't be advisable for you to wander off without permission. Ever. I have my orders, and they're not pretty."

Anna turned to retrace her steps. So Lesley Horn had her under guard. She might have known. He would return any day now to claim her soul for his own. He would not be true to her, of course. The old-timer had seen him with the women in town, and even in this confused tumult of campers, she had seen him flirting shamelessly with the kind of girls who followed such a crowd.

The budding plans, not yet developed, to take the wagon and start for New Mexico were nipped before they flowered. Yet nothing could soil today's blissful revelation. Her body might be imprisoned, but her spirit was free.

She felt the eyes of the spy follow her back to the perimeter of her campsite. *But there are other eyes, too.* She looked up. *God's eyes.*

Back in camp, Deana gave a deep gurgling laugh as if she knew what had transpired on this day. Tendrils of wet hair flattened on her tiny neck. She was beautiful, and Anna now recognized a little replica of her own self in the child. Others had noticed and commented on the resemblance. Deana must favor her mother, with none of her father's flaws to mar her beauty. She had the Elliott blue eyes. She wished Jason could see her.

Anna caught the baby up and buried her face on the child's soft stomach, tickling her with a blubbering blow of breath. Both laughed without restraint in the aftermath of joyous relief.

"You're mine! Deana, you are mine!" Anna cried. "You are my own sister's precious baby! God gave you to me and me to you. Whatever Lesley Horn does, he cannot take you from me! I love you so much that I would *die* for you!"

164

The happy child blew slobbery bubbles.

"Oh, I wish my sister could know that I am alive and that I am caring for her baby!"

Anna stopped and pondered, her eyes glowing with a faraway light. "Maybe she *does* know, Deana!" The child reached up to pat Anna's face.

A middle-aged woman, her hair scraped back tight, heard the sparkling laughter and frowned. Death had so recently stalked the family, bitter crying would seem more appropriate from that direction.

The frontier certainly told strange tales.

20

The Countdown

*B*lue-uniformed cavalrymen moved in across the river to be on hand for the big day and to keep the eager mob from pushing across the river before the long-awaited signal. The guarded land lay like green carpet beneath them with a backdrop of spring-clad valleys and timbered hills.

Once the date of April 22 was announced for the run, more wagons came, squeezing into every available space along the waterfront.

After her encounter with Lesley's informer, Anna stayed close to her own camp, but as the circle of wagons thickened, she felt closed in, smothered. The old-timer roved from camp to camp, a self-appointed ambassador of good will. He dropped by often to keep Anna up on all the news. By now he had learned her name and called her Miss Anna, running it together in a single word that sounded like "Mizanna."

"The government sent the troops here to keep the boomers out until opening day," she heard him say to Philip. "I have a copy of the law." He fished a crumpled paper from his pocket. "It says: 'No person who goes upon

167

said lands between the time of the issuance of the proclamation and noon the twenty-second day of April shall have any right to take any claims or derive any benefit from them.' "

"Yes, I heard about the law."

"I don't know of a soul who'd want to sneak in unfairly and dishonestly, do you, mister?" The old man looked at Philip, his leathery, wrinkled face a sober study.

Philip turned to some useless task and coughed.

"And I understand there's a long prison term for a body who false-swears they haven't entered the land when really they have."

"Um. Hum."

"Well, fair is fair, and I hope they catch everyone of them who go in sooner than they should. *Sooners* is what I call them. Just no-good *sooners.*"

Philip's face turned red.

"I heard that in some places, the government has set fire to the prairie to smoke out claim jumpers who slip in. I say it's a good idea. Don't you?"

A ridge of hard-set muscles framed Philip's jaw. Apprehension showed in his eyes. Since Esther's passing, he talked less and worried more. Anna wondered if the old man knew that Lesley Horn was one of his despised "sooners."

The old fellow ambled away, swallowed by the excited, seething camp. A clear-cut date brought unleashed optimism, and all around Anna people made happy plans for the future. Men pitched horseshoes to pass the time in the golden afterglow of sunset, their deep voices intertwined with the banter of the women and the prattle of playing children.

168

Someone shouted the date every day as the gap closed on Anna's single life. When her sparse-toothed friend called "ten more days!" she longed for an Old Testament Joshua to call a halt to time for her. Low, menacing storm clouds built in her soul, reminding her of the inward panic she always felt just before a vicious sandstorm on the Texas plains.

As the countdown started, the aged gentleman found something to report every day. He was as faithful as a daily newspaper and probably more accurate, Anna thought.

On the ninth day before the run, as Anna stoked up the campfire at daybreak, the shrill voice of a little old lady splintered the morning calm. She pointed and gestured. Across the river, several prairie schooners disappeared into the timber, their coach wheels still dripping water from their crossing.

"The posse! Get the posse!" the frantic lady called, rousing late sleepers. "There go some *claim jumpers!*"

The old-timer hobbled by at a near run. "Where? Where?" he shouted, shading his eyes. He looked the wrong direction.

"There! See!" She grabbed his arm.

The outcry brought the deputy and his thirteen-man posse to the chase. It was the theme of talk about camp all morning, the old man telling and retelling the story. Most of the objectors, Anna decided, merely raised a ruckus because they were not among the group that made the premature entry.

Before sundown, Anna had heard the entire account and could recite it by heart. "They found the men and wagons all right," the old-timer clapped his hands togeth-

169

er. "The wagons were parked four miles up in the territory with the men around a campfire eating! I'd call that nervy, wouldn't you, Mizanna? Makes you wonder just how many more have already slipped in there.

"Well, anyhow, there was a shootout, and several of the men were wounded. Twenty-five were taken prisoners, but the posse didn't know what to do with them. They had to build a makeshift prison to hold them temporarily. But there's already talk that they'll release them back to this side of the river and let them make the run with the rest of us. There's too few lawmen and too many rushers to keep everybody out! I hear there's other boomers camped in the woods and brush that they haven't found, hiding out with their land already picked."

"Yahoo!" A yell split the air.

"What's happened now?" The old man hurried away but soon came back. "Somebody's horse got loose from its picket rope and got across the line. I was wondering what they'd do in case something like that happened. If the owner goes over to get it, you see, he'll be breaking the law and will disqualify himself for any land. And no man wants to do that."

"So what will they do?" Anna asked.

"It was easy. They struck a compromise. The bluecoat said the owner of the horse could send his little boy over to fetch the animal back since the boy was too young to claim anyhow. There's generally a way out of any situation in life if you look hard enough. And when it's impossible, we can always turn to Somebody bigger to help us." Anna sensed a hidden message meant for herself.

On Easter Sunday, one day before the rush, the silver-haired old-timer took it upon himself to hold a religious service on the riverbank. He stood on a box and rang a cowbell for attention. Women, children and a few men gathered to hear his message. Anna took Deana and went along.

"We've come to a great day in our lives, brothers and sisters," he said. "Some of you will get land and some of you won't. All of us must accept God's times and His will for our lives. Blood will likely be spilled before this great land is settled. But remember, you won't win a lasting victory with a six-shooter. If you kill a man, you'll have your conscience to live with forever after."

Anna was certain she would never forget some of his wise admonition. People crept back to their wagons, subdued and thoughtful. The old-timer limped into Purcell.

The stream mirrored the fading crimson of sunset when he returned. "It was a bad day in town," he reported to Anna. "Cowboys and boomers rode the streets, firing their revolvers and passing the word that no one had better get in their way when they crossed the river tomorrow. I saw your man there in a sad state of revelry. I'm surprised he hasn't been shot full of holes already.

"This land rush is going to be one day in history that none of us will ever forget. Have you got your stick ready with your name on it?"

"No, sir."

"You'll have to have one. Everybody needs a name stick. When you cross the border and find ground that pleases you, just put your pole in the ground. Do you understand how it works?"

"Yes, sir."

"I'll make you a stick. And you'll want to tell your driver to watch that dry sand in the riverbed, Mizanna.

There's terrible quicksand spots that could swallow a whole wagon. You'll want to go across where there's a wide stretch of ground and a short span of water."

Anna said nothing and showed no interest.

"But at that, we've got it better than those crowding and cussing on the Kansas border. I hear there's no water up there. No place to wash, no place to sleep, nothing to eat. A cup of water sells for a dollar—and you have to stand in line for three hours to get one. Wouldn't be so bad, they say,if it was *drinkable* water, but it isn't. It's filthy tasting gyp water. So bad you can feel the alkali cake on your tongue. Yep, Mizanna, we're mighty blessed."

Anna looked down at her worn-out shoes.

"Your heart hasn't caught the Oklahoma fever, has it?"

"No, sir. I have land in New Mexico . . . if I could just get back to it."

"It might behoove you to do some praying tonight, Mizanna. You sure don't want to be yoked up with that young man who drinks and carouses."

"No, I don't."

"The government sent in Lieutenant Samuel W. Adair this evening to guard the main ford and the river bridge. Aye, but he's a handsome laddie, looking stately and regal in his blue and gold. Now there's a real man for you! He has a white horse like I've never seen! They say he'll be the one to give the signal. At *precisely* twelve o'clock noon tomorrow, it'll be."

The tired glaze in Anna's eyes made him cluck with sympathy. "Aye, Mizanna, you must get yourself some rest before tomorrow. You're all tuckered out, and that's

172

no way to face the big day in history. I'll bid you good night, and I will say a prayer for you ere my old head lays itself on my pillow tonight.''

For once Anna was glad when the old man finished his newscast and moved on to his dugout. She was in no mood for conversation. A blackness buried her, and she could not find her way out of it. Even her frantic heart-prayers refused to come to the surface.

Night fires burned low. Tomorrow would be the day.

Anna fumbled around in the wagon for clothing for herself and Deana to wear on the trip. She'd need her bonnet and her shawl.

But her bonnet and her shawl were not where she had laid them. She searched the tent and then the wagon. These items of clothing were missing. When had she last seen them?

21

The Land Run

*A*nna awoke in the dim gray hours of morning. A rooster warned that a new day approached. She tried to will herself back to sleep, to postpone the future.

This was the day of the intent race from the highways and byways by the rich, the poor, the refined, the ignorant—the day she had hoped would never come.

Dark figures moved to meet the long-awaited moment. The camp hummed with activity.

As the sun burst over the eastern rim of sky, turning the valley to silver and gold rainbows, a tonic air fanned down from the north, and the heavens were as blue as a summer day. Not a cloud smirched the sky, an ironic antonym to Anna's storm-wrenched heart.

"Such a spring-fresh morning!" greeted the old-timer, watching for Anna's smile and finding none. "Such a sunrise and sparkling dew! It is a perfect, glorious day for the run, Mizanna. Why, nature herself seems to be on her best behavior! And just look at those knee-high grasses and sweet flowers awaiting us. No wonder it's called the Promised Land. Now I know how the children of Israel must have felt when they looked across to Canaan. Reminds me of that old song about casting a wistful eye. . . . What's the matter, Mizanna?"

Tears clung like pearls to Anna's golden lashes. "I don't want to go. I'll never be happy . . . across the river. But I have to go through with it for . . . her." She bent and kissed Deana's head. "But, oh, I loathe the thoughts of a life with *him*. Life's such a long journey to travel a bumpy road."

"God will take care of you."

"Oh, sir, did . . . did you pray?"

"That I did, Mizanna. If the good Lord doesn't take your cross away, He'll give you grace to bear it. You know, the Lord never sends a trial our way that He doesn't weigh it and measure it before He lets it come to us. He gets out His rule and makes sure it isn't too long and then lays it on His scales to be certain it isn't too heavy. Look at me, Mizanna."

Anna raised her head. Her chin quivered.

"Our Father has promised us that He'll never put more on us than we can bear. And He said He'd give us some joy all along, too. All our tomorrows pass by Him to get to us. So trust Him."

"I'll . . . I'll try. I'm sorry to be a crybaby." She managed a thin smile. "And yes, it's a . . . good day for the run."

"That's a brave girl."

"Have you seen my slat bonnet, sir? I can't imagine where I must have mislaid it."

"Last I saw of it, it was on your head. I'm sorry you misput it, but the sun might do those peaked cheeks a favor."

176

The old-timer shambled off toward the river, enjoying the last-minute confusion of the camp: horses jockeying, wagons backing out, people pottering in a hundred unnecessary tasks. Camp breakers, preoccupied with final preparations, paid him little attention.

Later in the morning he came back to Anna. "Did you find your lost bonnet?"

"No, sir."

"I fetched you one from a lady that had two."

"Thank you!"

"Mizanna, you should see the train loaded and ready to cross the railroad bridge! There's more than twenty cars, all jampacked with men on top, hanging from the sides, on the steps, and even on the cowcatcher. Any place to get a footing! Some of the passengers allow they'll dive out the windows and have their baggage flung after them when they see a parcel of land they hanker for."

"I marvel that the little old lady who threw up such a protest about the claim jumpers doesn't howl about the unfairness of the train's ability to outdistance the wagons," Anna laughed.

"Oh, they've got that Sante Fe iron horse keyed down to the speed of a four-footed one. That's in the rules. Now, rail would be the way to go if you didn't get your neck broken in the jumping and the landing." He lowered his voice so that it would miss everyone's ears but hers. "Some do say that spies have been going in by train for weeks to scour out the country and learn its advantages for themselves. And unmolested by soldiers, too, it's reported. I'm a peacemaker and so I didn't advertise it. I can't figure people that don't want to play a game fair and square. My pappy taught me that it's not so much

177

the winning or losing as how you play the game."

Philip Horn came to hitch up the wagon, but Lesley was not with him. "It will be a wild ride, Anna," he warned. He nodded a dismissal to the old man. "I won't have time to see to your comforts. Can you manage with the baby?"

"I can manage."

"Lieutenant Adair allows that if the river was a whit higher than it is, passage would be impossible," offered the old-timer, lingering on. "And you want to watch those bogs of quicksand, mister. Death traps, they are."

Philip grunted, the sound barely audible above the rattle of stirrups and the creak of saddles.

"Fine man, that Adair," added the old fellow. He looked directly at Anna. "Fair man."

"We'll be moving closer to the water, Anna, to get our place," Philip said. He left the old man standing.

As the hours wore away to minutes, horsemen and drivers scurried to the river's edge to get a toe on the line. A thin picket of blue-suited soldiers faced the anxious human wall across the river.

At ten minutes before noon, a young soldier called, "Everyone on the line!" Anna looked around for the old-timer, but he was nowhere in sight. She supposed he was tucked away in a carriage somewhere.

Impatient people waited. They rode bareback, in open buggies, in light farm wagons, in carts and in racing sulkies. Anna saw a bicycle, the first such contraption she had ever seen. Some stood at the line devoid of beast or vehicle, ready to make the run on foot. There surely couldn't be enough land in the whole world, she decided, to apportion to this many people. Someone would be left out.

She would be glad for any of them to have her part and lot.

The lieutenant moved to the fore, calmly sitting on his white stallion. The old-timer's evaluation of him was correct; he was a handsome man. He held his stopwatch in his hand and began to count off the remaining seconds.

Anna braced for the jolt.

"Ten, nine, eight, seven, six, five, four, three, two, one." All movement and life hovered in suspense awaiting the signal. Like the prophetic angel of God commissioned to proclaim "time no more," the officer's timepiece held men's destinies suspended in these last dangling moments.

Lieutenant Adair raised his hand. The boom of a Winchester rifle thundered its report across the valley, and the emancipated throng went wild. That shot seemed to move the world, and Anna moved with it, clinging to Lesley's frightened child.

Behind her, whips cracked and men swore at their horses. A cloud of choking dust made breathing difficult. Spurred horses plunged ahead. Heavier wagons thundered by. The Horn wagon jerked and moved. Slowed. Lurched and rolled again. Anna braced herself, giving extra support to Deana's small back. She equated this tumult to a storm, one many times fiercer than a sand-sweeping demon of the plains. The inferno of moving, shoving objects seemed a nightmare too fearsome to endure.

She tried to look everywhere at once. Wagon poles snapped, axles broke, horses bucked. The deafening sound was like a roar of thunder. She was frightened and shocked.

Those on horseback paid little heed to those on foot. At the bloodcurdling scream of a young man, Anna caught

179

her breath and begged Philip to stop. The man had been thrown from his horse and was trampled under hundreds of sharp hooves. But Philip could not hear her. On he plunged in his mad race for land.

What had happened to the minds and emotions of these land-hungry people that they would show no regard for human life? Anna asked herself. It seemed to her that they had lost all judgment and reason except to achieve and attain their purpose. In some ways this day represented humanity at its worst.

Shouts, shrill cries, and blows mingled with the snorts and splashes of the horses as they flung themselves into the river and swam toward the opposite shore.

"Quicksand!" Anna heard a terror-filled woman's voice. Far to her right, a wagon floundered and went down. She remembered the old-timer's grim warning. *Worse yet,* she thought, *is the spiritual quicksand that I face beyond the river.*

On the sand banks behind them lay the body of a young boy. She had not seen him fall, but she supposed he was dead. Could she ever forget these scenes tattooed on her soul?

She turned her head from side to side to take in the fast-moving drama, the havoc wreaked by the storm. Only it wasn't a drama; it was real life: In they go, headlong. A horse falls into a deep hole. The rider falls. Another horse stumbles and falls on the man. There's a desperate cry, then a shout of victory. The man is safe. A horse breaks away, and his rider dives after him in the chest-deep current. Catching up to the horse, he pulls himself into the saddle. And on the cyclorama goes.

Shiny-flanked horses forged on, tails sometimes

afloat, sometimes under, fighting to keep their noses up. Strong, swimming mounts surged ahead; weak ones struggled and hung back. Anna found pity even for the laden animals, who nurtured their own instinct to survive. Was any piece of ground worth this outrageous price?

"John!" A man's urgent voice pulled Anna's attention to the left. "My pack is slipping! Never mind . . . Quick! Over there! There's a boy drowning. His foot is caught! Hurry!"

Anna saw that there was not a danger-free spot or moment in the churning river. Here and there a man left his disconcerted horse and slid into the water to gain the shore as best he could.

The Horn wagon reached a sandbar. From the deeper channel, horses pulled themselves to this shelf of land with soggy manes and tails, water trickling from their heaving sides.

The trauma of crossing lasted no more than ten minutes, but it seemed to Anna an eternity. The gaping wounds that cut into her sensitive nature would not heal quickly.

The land race, less tragic than the water crossing, had its strange scenery, too. Few contented themselves with stopping on the border. The land must be better farther on. One man, though, who crossed the line with a plow hitched behind his old horse, dropped the implement into the virgin soil and began a furrow around his claim as though he had been there for years. Anna reckoned that he would be the envy of some who did not find land at all.

A big red-whiskered man with a beard like a fork full

of hay busied himself carving his initials on the trunk of an oak tree. A lone woman in a faded calico dress and sunbonnet crossed the unfamiliar ford in a springless wagon. Her *Mayflower*. Where did she get her courage?

A pudgy, round-faced man, running and looking back over his shoulder, fell into a shallow well and couldn't get out. A passerby pulled him up.

Racers disappeared into woods and washes. Philip rushed on, goading his dirt-caked horses. Where was his destination? Wherever it was, Lesley had the stake set and would be hidden in the brush awaiting their arrival. She could never enjoy this land dishonestly captured.

A sharp-beaked hawk dove into a swale where the bushes might harbor a gopher or rodent. Something about the shiny black vulture reminded her of Lesley Horn. She shook her head to be rid of the image. She did not want to see whether the screeching bird caught his prey or not.

The old-timer shared her feelings about Lesley Horn. The old-timer said he would pray. The old-timer . . . aged, but not old. With whom had he crossed the river?

Where would he choose to build his sanctuary? If it could be close to her, perhaps she could lean on his faith to survive her meaningless marriage.

22

Left Behind

"*It's* useless to try to join the race!" muttered the old-timer. "I'm too old, too slow. The race is to the young." With eyes that yearned for younger days of strength and vitality, he watched the white canvasses of the schooners scatter and move off toward the horizon that cut the blue sky. "Looks like a fleet of beautiful ships sailing away home. My land will have to be in another world." He raised a hand with skin like parchment to wipe away a tear.

From his pocket, he pulled his fob watch, slid his thumb across its curved glass face as a matter of habit, and sighed. It was two o'clock. He watched as the last wagon pulled across the ford. Most of the others had already disappeared, leaving behind a prairie strewn with wrecks, smashed axles, and broken wheels.

He would miss the campers he had socialized with, especially Mizanna. She reminded him somehow of his own Rose. Perhaps it was her gentle nature, her guilelessness. The year he had traveled with his young wife by his side seemed to his misted memory a little slice of heaven on earth. They had been happy, too naive to believe their happiness could ever end.

When his Rose was plucked from him in an epidemic, his life lost all fragrance. Some men found only one true love in an earth span, while others went on to another affection, quite as blissful. While trying to decide into which category he fit, life slipped by until Rose loomed more angel than human in his hindsight and all earth's crop of women displayed feet of clay. He had found no Mizanna to replace his beloved Rose.

Mizanna. He gummed an unintelligible prayer for her that no one but God could have deciphered. How he wished she could be liberated from that philanderer! If he were choosing a mate for her, he'd choose a stalwart, respectable, true-blooded man—not a boozy idler. But he'd likely never see her again, never know her fate.

What could he do now that he had been left behind on the shores of the South Canadian River? The dreadful futility of the aged wrung his aspirations dry. He saw himself as he was, nothing but a spent and outdated relic of the past. He looked about, confused.

A young stranger on a heaving horse reined up. "Can I help you, sir?"

"They . . . left me. I can't . . . walk all the way." The words tumbled out as the old-timer pointed across the river to the lea sprinkled with debris.

The young man dismounted. "Here. Ride my horse. He'll be grateful for a lighter passenger. I'll walk. Just tell me where you want to go."

"You'll miss your land lagging along with an old man like me!"

The stranger held up his hand. "I'm young and I'm just here searching for someone. I don't want land."

"Who might you be searching after, lad?" the old fellow wheezed.

"The name is Horn. I need to find them right away."

"Oh, yes. Mr. Philip Horn, perchance? Camped right here they were until this very morning. One of the lady-folks died a few days ago. A pity it was and so close to land-claiming time, too."

The young man gripped the saddlehorn to steady himself. What if Anna had . . . lost heart and died? His mind shied from the thought like a spooked horse. "Do you . . . know her name, sir? The one that died, I mean."

"No. I'm not good on remembering anything anymore. I never wanted to admit to being senile, but my 'call back' don't always bring 'um back. I'm past my eightieth year, lad. The old mind lays down and snoozes when it ought to be working when you reach my age."

"What did she look like, sir?"

"Which one you mean?"

"The one that . . . died."

"My eyesight's poorly, too, young man. I can hardly see my own reflection in the looking glass to tell where my nose sits on my face."

"Was she *young?*"

"Mizanna, you mean? The one that was caring for the baby? No, sonny, it wasn't that one who died. It was the madam, the wife of the older man."

Jason let out his breath. He felt as though he'd held it in until his whole being was numb from lack of oxygen. Thank God it wasn't Anna who died! He could never have forgiven his mother—or himself—if she had passed on under the abuse of these uncaring people.

"Let me help you into the saddle. We'll move along

185

as quickly as possible. I want to see Anna before I return home.''

''Let's see now.'' The old gentleman puckered his face into a picture of thought, his chin almost reaching to his nose in the effort. ''When did she say she was to be married? Oh, yes, I recall now. She is to be married *tonight*. To the wee bonnie child's father.

''I suspected all along that the young scoundrel was already over in the territory hiding out, holding land illegally. He was as dishonest as sin. I saw him up in Purcell drinking and hanging out with those wicked women. It isn't fair what he did about the land, but a lot more of them did it, too. I don't know if he even knows about the old lady, his mother, dying. He didn't come back often these last few weeks. He didn't seem to hold much softness of heart for his mother, the baby, *or* his sweetheart! And for shame. She was such a guileless thing. These young bucks are 'without natural affection' just like Paul tells about in the Bible, don't you think? That young man is a wild bronc.

''I thought the Horn name fit him to a T. He'd look as natural with *horns* as the devil himself. It isn't any of my business, but it makes me sad to see such a gentle thing as Mizanna yoked up to such an untamed sort of rabble rouser. Don't believe you introduced yourself, young man. What's your name and your station?''

''I'm Jason Lewis, sir. I have inquired from camp to camp for Anna. I've been cursed at, pushed aside, and told by troops to move on, but I couldn't give up. I knew that Anna was out here somewhere in this boiling caldron of humanity in need of my help. Sir, I love Anna with all my heart and I have come for her. I don't think she real-

186

ly wants to marry . . . Lesley Horn."

"You're right, Mr. Jason Lewis. She doesn't want anything to do with that Horned creature. She the same as told me so. The only reason she was going through with the marriage is for the baby's sake. In fact, she asked a prayer of my old lips that the good Lord would send her a rescue from him."

Jason closed his eyes. If only he could have arrived one day sooner. Well, he would find her, and if she should belong to another, he would give her a brotherly greeting and return to West Texas. She need never know why he fought wind and weather to find her. He cleared the sweat from his forehead with his dusty hand.

"I don't know where they went from here, Mr. Lewis."

"I know the general direction. Mr. Horn told my father where he planned to homestead."

The old gentleman tried to pull his high-topped shoe from the stirrup. "Then go, young man! And hurry! Mayhap you can find her before tonight! Mayhap you're the answer to this old man's feeble prayers. I'll stay right here. I'm an old, used-up man and can't hope to live much longer anyhow. I'd gladly finish out my time right on this spot in starvation rather than see Mizanna chained to someone she is afraid of. She had a good heart, that one. Reminds me of my Rosie. Why, she'd have let me ride in the wagon right alongside herself and the baby if she had known I'd be left out."

"No, I won't leave you," insisted Jason. "If they left today, they can't be many hours ahead of us and it's early yet. We've several good hours of daylight left. We'll chance it together."

187

Jason and his charge soon caught up to the cavalrymen who followed the homesteaders to help in emergencies and to keep order. "You're late," one of the young officers grinned. "Won't be any land left when you get there."

"I'm not here for the land run," Jason explained. "I'm trying to get this old fellow up with the others. He was . . . somehow overlooked."

"Easy to do in this mob. And you?"

"I came . . . looking for my sweetheart."

The young soldier's mahogany brown eyes showed that he understood. "I'll take your friend and see that he gets where he wants to go." He gave a boyish salute. "You go on to your beloved. Do you know which direction she went?"

"They hoped to claim land between the river and Oklahoma Station."

"That way," pointed the soldier.

Jason nodded a thanks and hurried away, waving to the old man. He rode fast, passing buggies cracked up in gullies, buffalo wallows, and holes. A spring wagon, its shaft splintered, had been abandoned along with a surrey with a missing wheel. All of them, he suspected, told a story of broken dreams.

He hurried on, catching up with the rearmost travelers that straggled behind, hampered by heavier loads or crippled conveyances. He passed blushing-cheeked young maids and weary-faced older women with faded skirts trailing in the dust. They wore their hopes in their eyes. To these wives, mothers, and sweethearts, he thought, this must seem the final curtain call for a haven of their own.

He started to veer to the left to circumvent a spring-less buckboard driven by a solitary woman. The wheel of her vehicle hit a rock and bounced her trunk over the tailgate. Contents of the chest rolled in all directions.

Jason pulled hard on Jesse's reins, bringing him to a sliding halt. Another delay. But his gentlemanly nature would not allow him to ignore a lady in need of assistance. He gathered the calico-clad woman's uncaged treasures and returned them to the trunk. Then he lifted the box back into the wagon and rode off amid the profuse thanks that she did not know how to terminate.

How would he ever find Anna? Thousands of people made the trip. He would recognize the covered wagon and the horse when he saw them. But time was like a wolf. If he could but conquer this last enemy . . .

He bowed his head over the saddle horn and prayed one of the most urgent prayers of his life.

23

The Threat

Lesley Horn stood guard over 480 acres of prize land, a verdant cul-de-sac tucked in a horseshoe-shaped oasis outlined by an arroyo. This lush nook of nature included his land, Philip's land, and Anna's land. Philip would have passed him by, however, but for the sound of Lesley's voice.

"Right here, Father! You fool! You have a map. Can't you read it?"

Anna turned her head toward the voice but saw no one except a frumpy woman ready to shoo passersby from her claim. Then she looked again, not wanting to believe what she saw. Lesley, dressed in her own bonnet and long white shawl, stood defending the property in his disguise as an old lady.

"How do you like the ruse, old man?" he asked Philip. His loud guffaw added to Anna's embarrassment. She quailed at his utter disrespect. "Several wagons would have challenged our land, but they thought I was a weak little woman. Ha! Ha! How I fooled them!" He pulled a friendless rifle from beneath the shawl. "I didn't have to fire a single shot!"

He slung off the bonnet with a grimace of victory and dropped the shawl to the ground. Then he sprinted to the wagon and pulled Anna harshly to the ground. "I see you found another headpiece." He tried to kiss her, but she pushed him away. The smell of his breath left her queasy and faint.

"This is no way to welcome a future husband!" His inflamed eyes lighted with fresh anger. "Where's Mother? She has made me wait as long as I shall. This was her idea, but I'm not sure it was such a bad idea after all. If she tries to put me off again, though, I'll tell her . . ."

"Lesley!" scolded Philip. "Please get ahold of yourself and listen to me! We have some bad news."

"Not *you* now, Father! Anna is mine and I'm going to marry her tonight!"

"Your mother is dead, Lesley. We buried her beyond the river. I didn't know where to find you for the funeral. The old-timer that doubled as parson for the camp held a short service for her. I'm sorry we had to go ahead without you. She would have wanted you there. I wish we could have buried her . . . here."

Lesley showed no grief. "Then Anna will keep house for both of us. But I *will* kiss my bride-to-be!" He lurched toward her. "You will resist me no longer, you little trollop!"

"Lesley Horn!" barked Philip. "You will marry the young lady properly. It is what your mother would have wished, and it is what I wish. And the ceremony shall not take place until we have filed our claims. Otherwise the government will come in and lop off Anna's 160 acres."

"Then you will patrol our land while I take Anna with me to Oklahoma Station to file our claim and pay our filing fee right now. We'll be married while we are there. Now come, Anna.''

"You will act like a civilized human and help me un-hitch the team and get set up before you go anywhere," commanded Philip. "In fact, I demand that you not leave tonight. There's too much work to come by. Tomorrow is soon enough for you to get married. Some bully will push us off our land if we leave it unprotected tonight, and we'll have nowhere to live. You are foolish to think of leaving with all these wagons roving around looking for a place to bump off a landowner. After waiting years for my dream of owning Oklahoma land to come true, I don't plan to see that dream turn to ashes now. Get busy and help me set up here. That's the best insurance against losing this land we've worked so hard to get."

Lesley sulked and cursed and mouthed at his father, but as he sobered up, he became more reasonable. "Mother wouldn't have liked it here if she had lived," he said.

"Why?"

"Palm trees won't grow here."

"Bud told me anything would grow here."

"Bud was wrong. It's too cold here for California flowers or trees."

"Your mother would have loved it because I love it." Philip's tongue said what his heart knew was not true.

"And now I guess you'll be wife hunting."

"No. I won't take another wife. One woman around the place should suffice for the woman work."

"But you're never to forget she's *my* wife."

"You and Anna will take the child with you when you go in to be married tomorrow, won't you?"

"Absolutely not."

193

"I can't mother the land and the child, too. Besides, I don't know anything about babies."

"You can learn."

"What if she gets sick?"

"If she was the dying kind, she would have died before now. You couldn't kill that kid."

Wagons and horses passed, transporting pilgrims still looking for land. Lesley raised his gun when anyone looked his direction, and they moved on.

Caught in a cyclone of disgust and loathing, Anna took Deana in her arms and walked away from the wagon. *Any man that would pretend to be a woman . . .* "I will never marry—him!" she said with a fling of her head that dislodged her bonnet and set her hair loose. "Never."

"Oh, yeah?" Lesley stood behind her. She jumped.

"I'll . . . I'll *die* first." She turned to run but stumbled on a protruding root. Lesley grabbed her arm.

"You might at that." He narrowed his base eyes and doubled hard fists. "But you will not get away from me!"

"Lesley Horn!" yelled Philip. "Get yourself back here this minute and help me set up this camp for the night!"

Lesley turned back like a disobedient boy, spitting oaths.

"Let the girl have her walk, Lesley. She's tired from being cramped up in the wagon. It wasn't a pleasant ride for a lady. You'll have time enough to make your plans this evening around the campfire. And I forbid you to touch another drop of liquor today! Do you hear me?"

Tears glistened on Anna's feathery lashes. She had lost all hope of escaping the chains of an incompatible marriage. "Dear God," she prayed, "have mercy on me and my sister's baby." With such little faith, would the heartfelt words reach heaven or fall at her feet?

All my tomorrows must pass God's inspection before they can come to me. The old-timer had said it. Like a spring from a source unseen, strength seeped into her whole being, and she found herself singing a strange melody to Deana, sweet and low:

Sorrows must pass God's measuring rule
As well as each heartache and tear;
This is my weapon against Satan's tool
Of uncertain tomorrows I fear.

A lone horseman swept toward her, riding like the wind. She didn't lift her eyes. It would be someone looking for land, and if the land seeker tried to infringe on Lesley's "rights," he would be greeted by the barrel of a cold gun. None of it concerned or interested her. She and Deana had property much more valuable than this in a place where—according to Modeane's diary—the sun spent the winter.

The rider slid from his horse and hurried toward her. She started to run back toward the wagon, back toward Philip and Lesley, to escape this new danger.

"Anna!"

The voice . . . Who . . . ? Where . . . ?

"Anna! Wait! It's me . . . Jason."

"Jason!" A mingle of pleasure and relief rang in her voice and showed in her sunken eyes when she recognized him.

The glad look pleased Jason. He pursed his lips and motioned for her to keep silent.

"Oh, I know God sent you to help me, Jason!" she

whispered in a frantic rush to get the message to him. "You must help me and Deana get away from . . . *him!* He's taking me to Oklahoma Station tomorrow to be married. Esther is dead and I have legal rights to the baby. Let me tell you what I learned . . ."

"Stop!" The long gun barrel was pointed directly at Jason. "What are you doing here, Jason Lewis? You are a trespasser. Get off my property!" bellowed Lesley. "And NEVER COME BACK!"

"I've come for my girl, Lesley Horn. You knew she was mine all the time. I told you so the night of the sandstorm. I never dreamed you were yellow enough to force an unwanted marriage upon her. You promised me that you would never do that. Besides being yellow, you are a liar!"

Anna watched Lesley toy with the trigger of the gun. "Go, Jason!" she begged. "Lesley has been drinking. He will shoot you. Run for your life!"

A bullet whizzed past Jason's head. Anna thought she might faint. "Jason Lewis, you're a fool." Lesley gave a foul laugh and lowered his gun. "What have you to offer? That's your old man's horse you're riding. You haven't an inch of land to your name. And I would gamble a guess that you have no money. And look at this." He tilted his head from side to side in a mocking wag. "Acres and acres of virgin land covered by a dozen shades of green. Never been introduced to a plow. There's timber for a house, and I took money from an unlucky dead man." He drew a thick roll of bills from his pocket. "I'm going to be somebody. And Anna will be Mistress Somebody! Just watch our dust!" he spat at Jason in his contempt. "I'll fix Anna up like a lady! Now wish us a rip-roaring

196

honeymoon and get yourself out of here!" Lesley waved his fists and stamped the ground like a maniac.

"You can't buy love, Lesley Horn." Jason said it in an even voice, icy calm. Admiration for Jason's bravery brought pink to Anna's cheeks. He was tall, solidly muscled and much more handsome than she remembered from their years in the same household.

Sitting straight in the saddle, Jason turned to ride away to satisfy the pleading in Anna's eyes. His death could not help her. Lesley raised his gun to shoot Jason from his horse.

"Nobody but the scum of the earth shoots a man in the back!" The words, coming from Anna, were an indictment. "You have me and the child. The least you can do is let Jason Lewis go back to his family a whole man!"

Lesley's harsh fingers bit deep into her shoulder. "If he shows up again in the course of your lifetime—or mine—on my land or anywhere else, he is signing his death warrant. Do you understand?"

Jason had tried. Anna hugged the thought to herself. But what chance had a weaponless man against the marrow-chilling metal of a gun? She was glad he got off Lesley's land with his life.

24

The Babysitter

*T*he conversation Philip heard disturbed his upright soul. Why must his only son be such a fallen creature? Esther had defended him in her lifetime. She said let the wheat and the tares grow up together in one's life. But Esther's philosophy brought ruinous harvest and lacked righteousness.

The talk he heard was about the child. When Anna pleaded to take the baby along, Lesley retorted, "You can't dance with a tyke on your hip. You'll be the laughingstock of the dance hall."

"I don't . . . dance," the girl told him.

"You are marrying me now, Anna. Your goody-goody life is over. You will dance if I say so. As my wife, you are to make me happy. You can't please God without pleasing me because the Bible says for wives to obey their husbands. I might even have you do a little number on the dance floor for the sport of the cowboys down from Kansas. They'd like that and *I'd* like that."

"I won't," she insisted.

Philip didn't like the sound of Lesley's shallow, sardonic laugh. "You'll do," his son said. "I like your fire, your vinegar. I have always wanted to conquer a she-angel and dust her pretty wings with a bit of earth. The last one died on me before I succeeded. But you're stronger, spunkier. You'll last longer. And if you decide to check out too, there'll always be another to take your place."

Philip Horn frowned on that kind of talk. He'd been guilty of the sin of tolerance, but he was an honorable man. He found himself wishing that Esther had not insisted on the girl coming along as a nursemaid. She was no more Lesley's type than the first one. But then, without an influence for good in her life, what would become of the child? Or what would become of Lesley? Would Lesley settle down after the marriage as Esther predicted? These questions and others plagued Philip's soul and burdened his mind.

He watched Lesley and Anna leave. When the land was registered and the fee paid, no one could take their land from them. Lesley said he had the money to pay the fees for all three of them. Where did he get his money?

As they rode off, sympathy for Anna plucked at Philip's heart. Her stark, bonnet-framed face, set in grim determination, made a pitiful contrast to the delicate dress with its lace trim. The girl was doubtless still tired from the trip, but after the ceremony she could rest. Lesley was right to insist that she leave the child behind. She needed a release from that responsibility—which she took much too seriously—for a while.

Wasn't that the same dress Lesley's first wife had worn to her nuptial vows? Esther had given an exorbitant price for it at a fashion shop in San Francisco. Imported from overseas somewhere. Or was it New York? Esther was from another world, a softer world. He sighed. Lesley was right. Had she lived, she would never have adjusted to the primitive life here.

What had Lesley said about the marriage? Philip reached back for details to which he should have been more attentive. A parson was to meet them at noon in a hotel in Oklahoma Station to read their wedding rites. Normally a late sleeper, Lesley had sacrificed his laziness to arise at sunrise so that they might transact their business and not keep the minister waiting. Philip was glad Lesley had kept himself from his abominable jug so that he could apprise Anna of his plans in a logical manner. He noticed that Anna made no comment, offered no suggestions. She was an amenable sort, much like Lesley's first bride, humble and submissive. And the love she lavished on Lesley's child rivaled that of a real mother. Philip found that unusual. She must certainly love his son, Philip decided, to agree to wed him and rear his child.

Deana still sniffled in Philip's arms from her violent fit of crying. Sensing the moment of abandonment, she had clung to Anna with clawlike fierceness. Lesley, infuriated by Anna's devotion to the infant, had wrenched the child from her arms and had given the baby a frightening smack on her small leg when she cried for Anna. The actions of his hot-tempered son left Philip feeling helpless. How could he hope to comfort the child when he needed comfort himself? He wished he could cry, too.

Philip knew nothing of Jason's visit the day before. Occupied with making camp, he neither saw nor heard the brief fracas over Anna. When he asked Lesley about the gunshot, Lesley said that he shot at a skunk to chase him away. "We don't want skunks to start coming around." Sarcasm merged with hate. "So I figured the best thing to do was to put a bullet close enough to the critter's head to send him on his way without a stink."

Thus, when Jason rode up to the wagon a short while after the couple left for Oklahoma Station, Philip gave him a royal welcome. "Jason! It's a pleasure to see you here!"

"I can assure you the pleasure is mine." Jason smiled.

"Your sister left with my son, Lesley, not more than an hour ago," he said. "She'll be sorry she missed you, but you are welcome to camp here with me until she returns. I know you won't want to go on your journey without a visit with her. Anyhow, you'll help fill up my lonesome time here while they are gone.

"She'll regret that you didn't get here in time to travel with her to her wedding. It's always nice to have one's kinfolk to stand with them when they wed. You do know that she decided to marry Lesley, don't you? Esther said your sister posted you a letter. I suppose she told you of our whereabouts?"

"I left before the letter arrived."

"Then you didn't know about my wife's death?"

"I . . . heard."

"We're fortunate to have your sister to care for the baby. I honestly don't know what I would have done when Esther passed on if it hadn't been for Anna. I'm afraid Lesley would have been obliged to put the baby up for adoption. Neither he nor I know the first thing about rearing a child. Especially a girl child.

"Lesley's lucky to get a wife like Anna. She's a lot like his first wife. Not in looks so much as in her actions. Moves about like her. I always liked the first one, although she and Esther didn't have much in common. And I'll like this one, too.

202

"I don't know why all the young women take to Lesley. I'd be the first to grant that he's a bit wild. But Esther said he would settle with age. I hope he does. And I hope that he'll make a good brother-in-law for you."

"I may try to get to Oklahoma Station and be on hand for the ceremony."

"That would be nice! Did your family send you on up to claim some land for them?"

"No, I . . ." Jason fidgeted, his mind distracted from Philip's questioning. He was wasting precious time.

"Well, we got us a likely piece of property here. We have 160 acres for each of the three of us. Anna and Lesley will register us while they're in town. You might as well have a look around while you are here. I don't know that there would be any land left by now. It looked to me like there were more people than land sites. I just hope there was enough to go around."

"I . . . I just came to see Anna."

"I don't think you could get there in time for the wedding if you left right now. They planned to be married at high noon. A lot of good things happen at noon. The land run started at noon yesterday. I'll have a new daughter-in-law at noon today . . ."

The baby gave a shrill, high-pitched wail. "Oh, dear," Philip looked scared. "I can't tell if she is angry, hungry, or in pain. If I should let her die, Anna would never forgive me." He hunched his shoulders in a helpless gesture. "*She* wanted to take the baby with her, but Lesley wouldn't hear to it. Lesley left her in my care and I'm not handy with babies . . ."

"Would you like for me to take her for a little ride and quiet her, Mr. Horn?"

"Oh, would you?"

"I'd be glad to. And if I decided to go on to my sister's wedding, I could take her there with me. Babies love riding. They love horses. The movement puts them right to sleep."

"I'm almost . . . afraid . . . of children. I know so little about them—what they want and need. When Lesley was small, Esther wouldn't let me touch him! Babies seem so *breakable*. And they can't talk to tell us what their problem is."

"They're sturdier than you think, Mr. Horn. Just look how she has survived against all odds."

"The credit goes to your sister."

"I think that her wedding would be much more complete if the little girl is there. Of course, the little girl would never remember the occasion, but Anna could tell her about it in years to come."

"But I wouldn't want to ire Lesley. He wanted Anna to be free to dance."

"To dance?"

"To celebrate, you know."

"Well, I shouldn't think it would make Lesley any difference, if I am caring for the child, should it?"

"I shouldn't think so, but Lesley gets ticked off at the most trivial things. Why, yesterday he got mad at a *skunk!*"

"A skunk?"

"I heard a gunshot in the late afternoon and I asked Lesley what he was shooting at. I was afraid he may have fired at *somebody*. He said it was nothing but a dirty skunk and he shot near the skunk's head so the skunk would run without leaving a scent behind. That's what I mean by Lesley's unpredictable moods."

Jason crossed-examined himself. He thought of Lesley as a rat; Lesley thought of him as a skunk. The label fit Lesley quite well, but he hoped he never merited Lesley's evaluation of him. Better death than dishonor.

"That skunk may have come looking for a rat, Mr. Horn," he said. Then he took Deana and laid her tenderly on his shoulder. Her pitiful crying subsided.

"I think she likes you," Philip said.

"I love children. I'll take very good care of her, sir. And if Lesley gets out of sorts, I'll take all the blame. You go on with your work and have a good day."

Jason smiled at his good fortune. Getting Deana was simple enough. Now how could he reach Anna in time? He looked up at the sky. The sun stood directly overhead. He could not possibly cover the distance to Oklahoma Station and find Anna before . . . before . . . His mind would not supply the conclusion.

25

The Wait

*A*nna waited in the hotel lobby, feeling curious eyes upon her. Her hands fumbled with the lace at her neckline, wanting something to do to stop their shaking and fill their emptiness. How she missed Deana!

"Isn't she beautiful?" whispered a wealthy hotel patron to her friend. "See how the sunbeams play in her hair? The light makes it look like spun gold. My hair used to be that color. I think Rafael married me just for my hair! I accused him of it once, and he didn't deny it. And isn't that a lovely dress? And expensive! It wasn't bought around here in these cheap boutiques. Paris, maybe. Or New York."

"I believe someone could make a fortune with a shop in this embryo of a city. I predict that Oklahoma Station will be the capital of the Oklahoma Territory when it gains statehood. I say it's a pity we can't buy such gorgeous gowns here. I, for one, will welcome some sophistication. I'd like to attend a governor's ball. There's nothing but cheap dancing in these frontier towns!"

The woman who first spoke turned her attention back to Anna. "Her eyes look hollow and swollen like she's been crying. I wonder why she should be so distressed. You don't know who she is, perchance?"

"No, but I heard the desk clerk say that she was supposed to be married at noon. Her fiancé secured a room for them. But they had to wait in line to file their land claims and pay the fee. There's a crowd at the filing office today. That delayed them. The preacher has already come and gone. She's likely disappointed about the delay, but I think the man has gone to find the parson and fetch him back."

"I wonder if it might be Parson Dunn?"

"There's probably not more than one clergyman here, is there?"

"My Rafael knew the Reverend Dunn. Grew up alongside him up in Dodge City. Said he knew he would be a preacher or a lawmaker one, as bound and determined as he was that right would win out. Mr. Dunn's first name is Will, and Rafael tells a funny story on him. He says God said, 'Will you preach, Will?' and Will said, 'I will.' Rafael said the reason Will said 'I will' is so God could say, 'Well done, Will Dunn!' " Both women laughed. "The man that was here earlier . . . do you think he's the lucky groom?"

"Must be. He was a shifty-eyed and crafty one, wasn't he? Not at all the quality you'd expect for a well-bred lady like that one. I overheard the man at the desk say they both claimed 160 acres yesterday in the land run. Somewhere between here and Purcell. Then they filed their claims today before they wed so they could *each* claim land. If they had married before, they wouldn't have been allowed that much land, you see. That's fast thinking." She raised her plucked and penciled brows so high they disappeared beneath her low-slung hairdo.

"Well, I think I'll hang around for the wedding. I like weddings."

Anna stared out the window, seeing nothing, sensing nothing. An awful numbness paralyzed her emotions. Her tomorrow had come; it had somehow slipped by God unnoticed. She was sure it had not been weighed and measured. The lashing storm had struck, capsizing her dream. When Lesley returned with the preacher, life would be only a nightmare. Her mouth twitched. She would rather share a room with a poisonous viper than with Lesley Horn.

"Look!" pointed the pompous lady. "Each time someone comes in, she winces. She's hoping it's him each time, and then it isn't. Poor darling! She's probably afraid he's not coming back for her at all. And you just never can tell with these double-dealing frontiersmen. I surely hope he shows up soon."

Don't let Maw pawn you off. Jason's words came back to haunt her. That was before the sandstorm. The pawning off had come unexpectedly, before she could prepare for it. Before Jason could prepare for it. Esther Horn's shrewd plan seemed so judicious that it met with no opposition. Except perhaps from Jason himself, and that didn't count with his mother. Then had come the sandstorm that ushered her into this endless tempest. *So swift the storm. . . .*

26

The Tomorrow

*J*ason rode as fast as he dared with the child. The rocking motion of the horse soon put her to sleep. With the loss of sleep himself, he found it hard to stay upright in the saddle. All night long, he had watched the Horn property from a safe distance, ready to defend Anna against any unwanted advances of the half-drunk man. Thoughts of her jeopardy tortured his mind hour after weary hour, driving sleep from his eyes.

Anna. His sweetheart. He relived the suspense of the past when he found her after the Indian attack and took her to his home. To his mother. With less than noble motives, Corine took the child even though a childless couple wished to adopt her. Corine thought there would be financial rewards. The Elliotts were considered affluent. Then when Corine learned that the deeds to the Elliott property were lost, her interest in rearing the "stray child" (as she called Anna) waned. But by then, the couple who wanted her had relocated, and Richard Lewis had become attached to the orphan.

The old quarrel alternately festered and scabbed. The resentment that Corine harbored against the porcelain-white Naomi Elliott, her neighbor and landlord, included her light-skinned children. In fact, Jason reflected, his mother resented any fair-haired child. She had never forgiven the hapless ancestor who had mixed the family bloodline with Indian blood.

After the raid, Corine lived in terror of another, making life miserable for them all until Richard agreed to move her away. Corine argued against taking Anna to the high plains with them, but Richard's word prevailed.

Jason was careful to keep his affection from Anna as she grew older and lovelier, blossoming into a classic beauty that made him proud of her. Even in the pitiful attire Corine afforded her, she was pretty. Any show of sentiment on his part would cause his mother to seek ways to be rid of the girl. Jealousy was indeed as cruel as the grave.

When Anna left with the Horns, Jason's heart left with her. Even young Willy noticed that he wasn't the same. With his loss, he realized how much he had loved her and wanted to shield and protect her. Then when he kissed her cheek the day she left, he knew. He cringed at the memory: her small regal head . . . the crown of golden hair . . . the clear, trusting eyes. . . . She thought he had come for her. If only he had fled with her then!

For the first few days after she left, he convinced himself that the baby would not survive and that Anna would return. He waited and watched for her letter. It never came.

Driven by feelings he could not explain, he made a last trip to the post office in Lubbock, an idea nibbling at his mind. At the saloon, where he went to find the missing postal worker, he witnessed a senseless murder. A young drifter standing near him fell to the bullet, a mistaken target. He had done what he could to help in the mad confusion that followed. The postal worker had been injured, too, before Jason learned if a letter had arrived from Anna.

His heart would let him delay no longer. The nucleus of the idea grew into substance and took on the shape of a plan. Considering the date the newspaper gave for the Oklahoma land run, Jason knew he must go to the territory himself to determine Anna's welfare. That was his only hope of happiness.

Joshua, the smith's son, could be trusted to get word to his parents of his whereabouts so they would not worry about him. After all, he was twenty-three years old and able to care for himself. He hadn't time to lap back by his home, losing valuable miles and even more precious time.

Only while he rode toward her, the hours bringing him closer to her, did he find any peace. He slept as little as possible, utilizing the sunlight from dawn until dark. He'd lost more than a week skirting swollen rivers.

Now as he cradled the sleeping baby across his broad shoulder and swayed with the rhythm of the saddle, great tears gushed like fountains from his eyes. What had his efforts gained him? It was well past noon already, and she would be married by now. He had let her down. Better had it been for him to die at the hands of Lesley Horn and his savage gun than to live with the thought of the innocent girl wedded to that beast. His reason for not choosing death was the effect his assassination would have had on Anna. How could she live with a murderer?

If by a remote chance—dear God, grant that it be so—

the wedding had not taken place, he would fight for her to the finish. This time he would win or die in the endeavor.

Oklahoma Station had two hotels. Which would it be? Jason remembered the roll of ill-gotten bills Lesley had waved in the air. He would select the larger, more expensive lodge. Jason turned Jesse to the more imposing rooming house.

People on the streets stopped to look after the companionless man with a sleeping baby on his shoulder. He paid no heed to their stares. As if it was something he practiced every day, he tied his horse with his one free hand and hastened into the establishment.

At the desk, he asked after the list of recently registered guests. The day clerk opened the book and Jason felt something like the thrust of a blunt knife blade in his heart when he saw the inked entry: *Mr. and Mrs. Lesley Horn.* He supposed it was Lesley's penmanship. They were already married!

Anna sat in the straight-backed Duncan Phyfe chair, staring aimlessly out the window toward the railroad, but Jason did not see her. When he glanced about the room, her head was averted. He did not recognize her in the elegant gown.

He would have left without seeing her, but Deana gave a sudden small cry that brought Anna's head around with an involuntary jerk.

"Jason!" she cried. "You brought . . . my baby!"

Jason's eyes touched her, pleasure and pain fused in his face. He had done one last noble deed for her as a wedding gift. He had brought Deana to her.

The room fell silent.

214

"Is that the one she's to marry?" The stage whisper amplified in the sacred hush.

"No." The single word, with all it meant or didn't mean, gave Jason hope.

"Now that young man looks like her *kind,*" the whisperer judged. "I'd venture to say he's a real man! And such care he is taking of the infant. I wonder . . ."

Anna's deadened nerves tingled to life. Maybe this day hadn't been overlooked by God when He was weighing and measuring after all. She clutched Jason's arm, moving him toward the door. "Take me away, Jason. Hide me! Quickly! Before he gets back with the parson to say the vows! We haven't much time!"

In her reckless hope, Anna forgot that anyone else was in the room. She had eyes only for Jason. And Deana.

27
Another Kiss

"*A*nna, you've lost weight." Jason's arm, like a band of iron, pulled her and Deana up onto the horse with him. She felt the stretch and ripple of his muscles. "You and the baby together won't weigh a hundred pounds."

He held her as easily as she held Deana. Her tumbled hair fell loose and blew across his face and lips. Holding the child and her small gripsack, she could not reach the flying mass to tame it. The dancing strands played across his cheek. Except for the sounds of the wild rush about her, it would have seemed a fantasy. Even so, it was hard to believe that she had eluded Lesley.

"When I am . . . free, I can eat again." A note in her laughter suggested hysteria. Jason pulled her close to his chest and held her.

They said little until they were out of the town, and then Jason spoke. "I want to get out of this territory before dark. This is no place for a lady. And Lesley Horn will surely try to follow us."

"He won't be able to find us, will he?"

"I'm not worried about you and me, Anna. I'm worried about the baby. The child belongs to Lesley. If we are caught with her, we could be charged with kidnapping. If I am convicted, I will be put in prison. I don't mind for myself, but I can't help you if I am locked up."

"I'm going to seek legal custody of Deana. She is my nearest blood relative."

"You haven't any living relatives, Anna." Jason's voice held sadness and offered sympathy. "I wanted to tell you before, but I didn't dare. You belonged to a family named Elliott. They were all killed in an Indian raid on the New Mexico border when you were very young. We lived nearby. I found you . . . asleep in the house."

"When I didn't find my name in the Bible you brought, I knew I didn't belong to your family. You got my letter, didn't you?"

"No. I didn't get a letter. I went to the post office before I started this direction, but ran into some difficulty getting the mail. But no matter now. I'm glad I didn't get it."

"I'm glad you didn't, too."

"It brought me to you faster."

"Oh, but you are in for a surprise, Jason! After I wrote to you, Mrs. Horn died and Mr. Horn asked me to clear out the family trunk. I found a diary that Deana's mother kept before her death. I learned that Lesley was married to my own sister, Modeane Elliott."

"Modeane Elliott? But . . ."

"In the journal, she told how she escaped from the Indians and made her way to a wagon trail where someone found her and took her to California with them."

"How did you know that Modeane was your sister?"

"She had our family history all written down. There

218

could have been *two* Anna Michelle's, but she told about you, too!"

"About me?"

"Jason Lewis—her childhood sweetheart. The puzzle fell together, and I knew I was her baby sister."

"She was a lovely lass but above my social class. Your family was well-heeled and mine was poor."

"When Modeane grew up, her foster family arranged her marriage to Lesley. I think that he probably abused her and shortened her life. And he hoped that her baby wouldn't survive to haunt him. He has never shown the child any interest. Had we left Deana behind, he would have given her away to anyone who would take her off his hands."

"And you have proof that your sister, Modeane, was married to Lesley Horn?"

"Yes. I have her marriage certificate."

"That will do."

"I named her baby Deana in her memory."

"I like that name."

Back at the river, the soldiers made camp and prepared dinner for the womenfolk who had stayed behind until their husbands found land. Army men helped those with broken wagons. The young officer motioned to Jason to join them. "I see that you found your sweetheart! Join us for chow!"

Jason brought Anna a bowl of fish soup but ate little himself. He watched with anxious concern as the shafts of gold sank lower in the trees. The officer sensed Jason's anxiety.

"There's a nice hotel in Purcell," he suggested. "About four miles from here. It's fine enough for a lady.

And it's *safe* enough."

Jason shoved his hand into his near-empty pocket and said nothing. Hotels took money.

"Tell Mrs. Augusta Wright that Adair sent you and to lay the charges to me," he said. "The lady and the baby need rest." He squatted on the ground to draw Jason a map in the dirt.

Jason loathed charity, but Anna and the child must have rest before they could travel on to . . . to where? He could go little farther himself. "Just so Anna and the baby have a room," he said. He could sit the night through anywhere. With the river between Lesley Horn and the girl he loved, he could breathe more freely.

The old-timer limped up, holding his cane high in a sign of victory. "Say, laddie, I decided to join this army. Let the younger ones fight over the land. I'm too old to start over now. I'll help keep law and order. Army boys need a good sermon now and then." The lieutenant winked at Jason and Anna.

"And who's this be-yoo-tiful lady you have with you, laddie? I was hoping you'd find Mizanna."

"This is Anna, sir!"

The old man squinted doubtfully. He moved closer for a better view. "Mizanna!" he shouted. His cane tap-danced on the caliche. "Well, bless my soul, God *did* perform His greatest miracle. He weighed and measured all those tomorrows, didn't He? And He sent 'um out just right!"

They left the camp, followed by cheers and good wishes. But the black cloud that settled over Jason puzzled Anna. Her own spirits soared to cosmic heights. Why was Jason morose?

"Is . . . is something wrong, Jason?"

"I've been thinking on what Lesley Horn said. He was right. I have absolutely nothing to offer a lady, a wife. No money. No land. Not even a horse to call my own.

"Oh, I could have plenty if I wanted to play a crooked game. All over the West, ever since the War between the States ended, men have come to Texas to find unbranded cattle. One can grow rich with a branding iron. It's a fast way to build a herd, an empire. But dishonest. Most of those cattle belong to another rancher. Rustling, it's called.

"I'm penniless, but I could not bear to see you married to . . . him. The fact that I rescued you from him in no way obligates you to me. There'll be an honest man for you somewhere. And we'll find him!"

"Oh, but I . . . I . . ." Anna blushed. "It doesn't bother me that you have nothing of this world's goods."

"Need I tell you that you will not be welcome in my mother's house now?"

"Then I'll . . . I'll do something." Tears welled up, breaking over the dam she had built against them in her heart. "I don't want to cause problems for you and your family after you risked so much to . . . save me."

"I'll take you wherever you wish to go."

"What was my family's home in New Mexico like?"

"It was a very nice ranch house."

"Was it destroyed, too?"

"No, the house was untouched. The warring Apaches were frightened away by . . . something."

"Then we'll go there."

"As the only surviving Elliott, the property is yours if you can prove ownership."

221

"I have the deed to the property here." She patted her gripsack. "Lesley never knew Modeane had it. There will be no shortage of funds to rear Deana. The land is oil rich."

"You should be safe enough there now. The Indian massacres are a thing of the past." The light faded from Jason's eyes.

Anna's cheeks blazed with a girlish thrill. "Do you remember the kiss you gave me, Jason?"

He hung his head. "Yes, I'm . . ."

"I've relived it so many times that it must be ready to retire. I . . . need another one."

"You mean . . . are you saying . . . ?"

"I love you. And I hope that you can love both of us— me and Deana."

Jason stopped the horse. "Darling, you'll have your kiss right now." But the kiss found her soft lips instead of her cheek.

And it lingered while all the earth swam in a dizzy spin.

Then Jason bent to kiss Deana's downy head, too.

28
Storm's End

*N*oisy crickets sang Jason to sleep. Fatigue glued his eyes shut. He asked for a room for Anna and the baby, but his manly dignity would not let him take one for himself at the lieutenant's expense. In the ancient straight-backed settee, he slept sitting up.

"There you are!" The voice that telescoped in from some outside region hauled Jason across the sea of slumber to the shores of consciousness. His eyes flew open. He was sure that he had slept but a few minutes. A gas lantern thinned the darkness. Was it just after dusk or just before daylight?

"Lesley is looking for you and Anna—and his daughter. He is known in this town, and he will have you locked up in the calaboose for making off with his child. Lesley has no mercy."

"But sir, I . . ."

Philip checked Jason with a raised hand. "Now, it isn't me, son. I argued all the way here that the babe would be better off with Anna wherever she took herself. I hate to say it of my own flesh and blood, but he isn't fit in his fallen state to raise a child, with his weakness for drink.

But it's his way of getting even with the girl for giving him the slip in Oklahoma Station. He knows the only way he can hurt her is through the little one. Her heart is knit to the child as if it were her own. And then, if Lesley can see *you* caged up, he knows he'll have her back for himself. I'd say it's for his wounded pride he's hostile, more than for love."

"I'll be glad to talk to the deputy, sir. Anna has legal claim on the child and plans to file for custody."

"I hardly see how it would stand up in court, Anna not being a blood relative."

"Your son's first wife was Anna's sister. Deana is her own niece."

"Wait a minute, son. You are confusing me. Anna is *your* sister."

"No, Anna is no kin to me. She was the youngest of the Elliott children. I found her in the family home after an Indian raid, and my family took her in. She was scarcely more than a baby herself. We didn't know Modeane survived."

"Yes, I heard my late daughter-in-law speak of the terrible raid. Did . . . did my wife know all this before she died? Did Esther know that Anna was Modeane's sister? Is that why she was bent on Lesley marrying Anna?"

"No, sir. Anna found a diary that belonged to her sister packed away in an old trunk in your wagon after your wife passed on. Anna feels that, since the baby belonged to her sister, she would have some rights."

"That would be my thinking, too, but Lesley is like a bear robbed of cubs. He'll find a way to be rid of you and get Anna back. And he'll be here any time now. I would suggest that you get your . . ."

224

"Sweetheart."

". . . whatever—and get out of here."

"What time is it, sir?"

"The sun set about two hours ago. But there'll be a moon to travel under tonight."

"I'll . . . awaken Anna and we'll . . . leave."

"I would advise it."

Jason knocked on Anna's door. "It's me, Anna. Jason." There was no response.

He waited. Had Lesley Horn already found Anna and taken her away? Fear ate away at the lining of his newfound hope. He put his ear to the door, but could hear nothing.

"Anna!"

Her sleepy head and robed shoulders appeared at the door. "Is it time to go already?"

"Yes, dear! Philip Horn is here and . . ."

Anna clutched the door facing for support. "Philip Horn? Oh, Jason! Is Lesley here, too? I can't . . . we can't lose each other now!"

"I feel the same way about it, love. That's why we must flee. Lesley will be here any minute. Get dressed quickly and bring Deana. We'll run . . . again."

"Will we ever stop running, Jason?"

"Yes, darling."

"Shall we . . . slip out the window?"

"Yes, Mr. Horn suggested we try to get out ahead of Lesley . . . if we can. If Lesley find us, he'll have me thrown in jail."

"Mr. Horn has a good heart. I'll hurry!"

Jason slid out the tall window first and took the baby that Anna handed down. Then Anna gathered her skirts about her and dropped to the ground.

"If we can get back to Lieutenant Adair, Anna, we can hope for some protection," Jason said. "I consider him a friend. Thank God for moonlight. The night will get brighter as we go." He put his arm around her. "Don't be afraid. God is with us."

They moved soundlessly along the shaded eves of the building. Neither of them saw Lesley Horn until he pushed the barrel of a pistol into Jason's ribs. "Don't move!" he warned.

Anna struggled against a blackness that filled her head. She couldn't faint now! She willed herself to take deep, metered breaths.

"You will both do as I say." Lesley had been drinking but was not intoxicated. "I am glad to see that you wore your wedding dress, Anna, because you will need it tonight. You will be married, like it or not. This is your wedding night, written in the stars for you, and I'm sure you will never forget it.

"We stood the parson up back in Oklahoma Station. Now I'm glad we did. This wedding will be even better because we've got Jason Lewis here for the ceremony." He turned the gun on Jason. "Face her and say you love her or I'll turn you to a corpse."

"I love you, Anna." Jason's soul was in his words. If this was his first and last time to utter those syllables, they would be the most beautiful, spoken with a devotion that no weapon on earth could kill.

The gun focused on Anna's head. "You do the same."

Anna's words warbled out, and Jason returned a trace of a smile. He understood.

"And I'm glad you've brought the kid. If you hadn't,

I would have sent you back for her. She will go along to the wedding . . . and after that she'll be out of my life forever!"

He looked around. "Bootsy!"

From the shadows, a full-lipped, tawdry woman with a low-cut costume moved to Lesley's side. In a quick move, he dropped the gun into a holster at his side, took her in his arms, and gave her a soggy kiss.

He released the buxom girl and turned to Anna. "Miss Holy-Holy, I want you to meet my new wife, *the* Mrs. Lesley Horn. We were married tonight. I got my fill of you. You were my mother's idea of a spouse for me instead of my own all the time. Something of your ways tattles of my first wife. She was my mother's notion, too, but I'm a big boy now, and it's time I live my own life. You had your chance and you missed it! Tough luck for you. I have the money, the looks, and the land. That mouse has nothing!" He curled his lips into a scornful sneer. "And I'm going to *make* you marry him!"

He pulled out the gun again and waved it in the air. "The preacher just finished up his church service around the corner. He did my vows and I'll see that he does yours, too. Ha! I'll even *pay* his fee to marry you off to that penniless pauper. It'll serve you right—and be my sweet revenge."

He pushed his chin forward and stretched his neck. "And you'll take the baby as a part of your punishment for skipping out on me. I hope you dance into eternity with that baby on your hip! You're stuck with her, see? Ah, but getting even feels grand! Now march to the parson or I'll shoot both of you on the spot!"

Lesley marched them, military fashion, to the storefront church. "Brought you some more customers, Preacher," he roared. "Tie the knot good and hard, because we don't want any slips in this one. Me and my new mistress will stand in as witnesses to make sure you do it up right. And I'll pay you well for your trouble!"

After the abrupt ceremony, Lesley Horn and his gaudy girl drifted off into the night, arm in arm.

The surpressed mirth, held rigid behind dole faces, ruptured into peals of joyous laughter when Anna and Jason started back toward the hotel. "I'll take my *punishment* now, ma'am." Jason straightened his face and tried to look solemn. "In the form of a kiss." His lips met hers.

"Jason, do you remember the sandstorm that started all this?"

"I remember."

"And the perfect morning after the storm?"

"It would have been perfect if Lesley Horn hadn't been casting possessive eyes upon my future wife!"

"The storm is over." Beams from the new moon caught in Anna's eyes. She snuggled close to Jason. "Our perfect day is dawning."